WARRIOR • 150

CARTHAGINIAN WARRIOR 264–146 BC

NIC FIELDS

ILLUSTRATED BY STEVE NOON
Series editor Marcus Cowper

First published in Great Britain in 2010 by Osprey Publishing
Midland House, West Way, Botley, Oxford OX2 0PH, UK
44-02 23rd St, Suite 219, Long Island City, NY 11101, USA
E-mail: info@ospreypublishing.com

© 2010 Osprey Publishing Ltd.

All rights reserved. Apart from any fair dealing for the purpose of private study, research, criticism or review, as permitted under the Copyright, Designs and Patents Act, 1988, no part of this publication may be reproduced, stored in a retrieval system, or transmitted in any form or by any means, electronic, electrical, chemical, mechanical, optical, photocopying, recording or otherwise, without the prior written permission of the copyright owner. Enquiries should be addressed to the Publishers.

A CIP catalogue record for this book is available from the British Library.

ISBN: 978 1 84603 958 4

E-book ISBN: 978 1 84603 959 1

Editorial by Ilios Publishing Ltd, Oxford, UK (www.iliospublishing.com)
Cartography Map Studio, Romsey, UK
Page layout by Mark Holt
Index by Alison Worthington
Typeset in Sabon and Myriad Pro
Originated by PDQ Digital Media Solutions, Suffolk, UK
Printed in China through Worldprint Ltd

10 11 12 13 14 10 9 8 7 6 5 4 3 2 1

ARTIST'S NOTE

Readers may care to note that the original paintings from which the colour plates in this book were prepared are available for private sale. The Publishers retain all reproduction copyright whatsoever. All enquiries should be addressed to:

Steve Noon,
50 Colchester Avenue,
Penylan,
Cardiff,
CF23 9BP
UK

The Publishers regret that they can enter into no correspondence upon this matter.

THE WOODLAND TRUST

Osprey Publishing are supporting the Woodland Trust, the UK's leading woodland conservation charity, by funding the dedication of trees.

FOR A CATALOGUE OF ALL BOOKS PUBLISHED BY OSPREY MILITARY AND AVIATION PLEASE CONTACT:

Osprey Direct, c/o Random House Distribution Center,
400 Hahn Road, Westminster, MD 21157
Email: uscustomerservice@ospreypublishing.com

Osprey Direct, The Book Service Ltd, Distribution Centre,
Colchester Road, Frating Green, Colchester, Essex, CO7 7DW
E-mail: customerservice@ospreypublishing.com

www.ospreypublishing.com

CONTENTS

INTRODUCTION	4
CHRONOLOGY OF MAJOR EVENTS	7
THE CONSTITUTION OF CARTHAGE	12
THE ARMIES OF CARTHAGE	15
RECRUITMENT	26
EQUIPMENT AND APPEARANCE	31
Spear . Sword . Dagger . Javelin . Sling	
ON CAMPAIGN	43
Salary and sustenance	
EXPERIENCE OF BATTLE	53
GLOSSARY	61
BIBLIOGRAPHY	62
INDEX	64

CARTHAGINIAN WARRIOR 264–146 BC

INTRODUCTION

With the defeat of Taras (Tarentum to the Romans, present-day Taranto), according to Florus, the poet and friend of the emperor Hadrian, 'all Italy enjoyed peace' (*Epitome*, 1.14.1). Peace, however, would be short lived, as the Romans were about to step over to Sicily, which was the first country beyond the shores of Italy on which they set foot, and cross swords with a potential rival in the western Mediterranean, the great Phoenician foundation of Carthage.

Carthage was the Semitic superpower that struggled with Rome in a series of three epic wars (264–241 BC, 218–201 BC and 149–146 BC), a titanic struggle that would lock the two cities into a 'Hundred Years War'. Probably the largest conflict of the ancient world, the Punic Wars, as history has named them, marked an important phase in the story of Rome and the rise of its empire. Before the first war, Rome was still a purely Italian power, not even in control of northern Italy. During the second war Hannibal had destroyed its armies and overrun the Italian peninsula. After the last, with Carthage a smoking ruin,

Qart Hadasht, 'New City' as the Carthaginians called it, was *Karchedôn* to the Greeks, *Carthago* to the Romans, and hence Carthage to us. The site was well chosen. It was naturally strong, situated as it was on what was normally a lee shore at the head of a promontory. The site's landward, western approaches consisted of the narrow neck of this promontory, which overlooked a marine bay to the north and a small azure lagoon within a large natural harbour, the present Bay of Tunis, to the south. This is an oblique aerial view of the site of Carthage. (Ancient Art & Architecture)

Whatever the subject, be it the grain supply, the coinage or citizenship, Marcus Porcius Cato (237–149 BC) always managed to relate it to Carthage and end his address with the same idiomatic expression: *'Censeo etiam delendam esse Carthaginem.'* This translates as 'It is my firm opinion that Carthage must be destroyed' (Plutarch, *Cato major*, 27.2). This image shows Punic houses on the slopes of the Byrsa, Carthage. (Pradigue)

its writ effectively ran from the Levant to Iberia and from the Alps to the Sahara. That, however, is not part of our present interest.

Carthage, at the time of the first war with Rome, was the greatest power in the western Mediterranean. Its wealth was proverbial, with Polybios (18.35.9) claiming that Carthage was the richest city in the Mediterranean world even when it fell in 146 BC, despite the fact that it had been deprived of its overseas territories after the second war and reduced to a second-rate power. Originally one of many landing sites and trading stations established by Phoenician settlers, Carthage had been founded even before Rome was only a huddle of huts and hovels squatting by the Tiber. According to Timaios of Tauromenion (*FGr Hist*, 566 F 60) the settlers pitched up in 814 BC conveniently near the mouth of the river Bagradas (Oued Medjerda), having sailed directly either from the metropolis of Tyre, one of the leading seaports of Phoenicia, or from the next-door colony of Utica, founded earlier by the Phoenicians. The Sicilian-Greek Timaios lived in the 3rd century BC, a time when it was still possible to draw directly on Punic sources for information, but the archaeological evidence is still short of this traditional foundation date, the earliest deposits found in the sanctuary of Tanit, the tutelary goddess of the city, belonging to 725 BC or thereabouts. Whatever the true date, Carthage was destined over time to take the place of Tyre at the head of the Phoenician world of the west, and in the process acquire sufficient power to become a rival on equal terms first with the Greeks and then with the Romans.

By the time of the outbreak of the first war, Carthage controlled the whole coast of northern Africa from Cyrenaica to the Atlantic, partly through its own colonies, partly through having taken under its aegis other Phoenician colonies, such as Utica. Though numerous, these colonies were mostly quite small, surviving because the coastal region was apparently otherwise sparsely inhabited. The eastern limit of the Punic empire had been pushed to a place the Romans called Arae Philaenorum, translated as 'Altars of the Philaeni' (El Agheila, south-west of Benghazi), which marks the boundary between

A divine couple, Tanit and Baal Hammon, gained a position of supremacy within the Carthaginian pantheon, a phenomenon plausibly connected with the political upheavals following the debacle at Himera (480 BC). In some texts the goddess, who usually had dominance over Baal Hammon in Carthage, is addressed as 'mother', but she is more frequently referred to as 'Mistress' or 'Face'. This is a limestone votive stele (Paris, musée du Louvre, AO 5250) from Constantine, from the 2nd century BC, dedicated to Tanit and Baal Hammon. We see the disc of the sun, the crescent moon, the hand raised in prayer, the Egyptian *ankh* ('sign of Tanit') and the caduceus. (Fields-Carré Collection)

present-day Tripolitania and Cyrenaica in Libya. To the west, Carthaginian influence extended beyond the Pillars of Hercules, as the Straits of Gibraltar were then called, and down the west coast of Africa at least as far as what is now Mogador in Morocco (Polybios, 3.39.1).

Beyond Africa, Carthage probably already controlled a few outposts in Iberia, which, like itself, had been originally founded by the Phoenicians, including Gadir (Cadiz) and Malaka (Málaga). In the Balearic Islands there were entrepôts on the southern coast of Ibiza, the best-known being Ebusus (Ibiza Town), and there was a string of such settlements around the coast of Sardinia, including Caralis (Cagliari). In Corsica Alalia (Aleria), at least, was in Carthaginian hands, while the Lipari Islands provided a safe anchorage for the navy. In Sicily Carthaginian power had been a feature for centuries, albeit of a chequered quality.

CHRONOLOGY OF MAJOR EVENTS

814 BC	Traditional date for foundation of Carthage from Tyre.
753 BC	Traditional date for foundation of Rome by Romulus.
574 BC	Tyre falls to Nebuchadnezzar of Babylon.
535 BC	Carthaginian–Etruscan fleet engage Greeks off Alalia.
509 BC	Traditional date for expulsion of Rome's last king.
508 BC	First treaty between Carthage and Rome (according to Polybios).
496 BC	Latin League defeated by Romans at Lake Regillus.
480 BC	Carthaginians defeated by Greeks at Himera.
474 BC	Etruscan fleet defeated by Sicilian Greeks off Cumae.
409 BC	Carthaginians capture Selinous and Himera.
406 BC	Carthaginians capture Akragas and Gela.
405 BC	Carthaginians fail to take Syracuse (peace accord with Dionysios).
397 BC	Dionysios captures Motya.
396 BC	Carthaginians retake Motya (foundation of Lilybaeum); Carthaginians capture and destroy Messana; Carthaginians lay siege to Syracuse ('plague' destroys Carthaginian army).
392 BC	Armistice between Carthage and Syracuse.
390 BC	Romans defeated at Allia; Gauls sack Rome (387 BC according to Polybios).
348 BC	Second treaty between Carthage and Rome.
344 BC	Timoleon of Corinth arrives in Sicily (revival of Greek Sicily).
343–341 BC	First Samnite War: a war invented by Rome?
341 BC	Timoleon defeats Carthaginians at Krimisos.
340–338 BC	Latin War: Rome versus its allies.
326–304 BC	Second Samnite War: Romans face mountain warfare.
321 BC	Romans humiliated at Caudine Forks.

316 BC	Agathokles takes power in Syracuse.
311 BC	Agathokles defeated by Carthaginians in Sicily.
310 BC	Agathokles lands in Africa.
307 BC	Stalemate between Agathokles and Carthage.
306 BC	'Philinos' treaty between Carthage and Rome.
298–290 BC	Third Samnite War: old foes fight back.
295 BC	Romans defeat Samnites and Gauls at Sentinum.
289 BC	Death of Agathokles.
281 BC	Rome declares war on Taras.
280–275 BC	Pyrrhic War: Rome versus Pyrrhos of Epeiros.
280 BC	Romans defeated at Herakleia.
279 BC	Romans defeated at Asculum.
278 BC	Pyrrhos sails to Sicily.
275 BC	Pyrrhos defeated at Malventum (renamed Beneventum).
273 BC	Latin colonies at Cosa and Paestum.
272 BC	Taras falls to Romans (end of pre-Roman Italy).
270 BC	Romans recapture Rhegion.
264–241 BC	First Punic War: Rome takes the path to empire.
264 BC	Roman alliance with Mamertini (consular army lands in Sicily).
263 BC	Hiero II of Syracuse becomes ally of Rome.
262 BC	Romans lay siege to Akragas.
261 BC	Akragas falls; Carthaginian navy raids Italy.
260 BC	Roman naval victory off Mylae.
258 BC	Roman naval victory off Sulci.
257 BC	Roman naval victory off Tyndaris.
256 BC	Roman naval victory off Ecnomus; Regulus lands in Africa (captures Tunis).

255 BC	Xanthippos defeats Regulus near Tunis (Regulus captured).
254 BC	Romans capture Panormus.
250 BC	Romans lay siege to Lilybaeum.
249 BC	Roman naval defeat off Drepana.
247 BC	Hamilcar Barca lands in Sicily (seaborne raid on Bruttium); birth of Hannibal Barca.
246 BC	Hamilcar occupies Heirkte.
244 BC	Hamilcar shifts to Eryx.
241 BC	Roman naval victory off Aegates Islands.
240–237 BC	Libyan War: Carthage versus its mercenaries.
238 BC	Rome annexes Sardinia.
237 BC	Hamilcar sent to Iberia.
231 BC	Roman embassy to Hamilcar.
229 BC	Death of Hamilcar (succeeded by Hasdrubal the Splendid).
229–228 BC	First Illyrian War: Roman 'police action' against Queen Teuta.
227 BC	Number of praetors raised to four (Sicily and Sardinia–Corsica made Roman provinces).
226 BC	Roman embassy to Hasdrubal (signing of Iber treaty).
225 BC	Romans defeat Gaulish invaders at Telamon.
221 BC	Hasdrubal assassinated (Hannibal Barca acclaimed generalissimo).
219 BC	Second Illyrian War: Demetrios of Pharos knocked down. Hannibal storms Saguntum.
218–201 BC	Second Punic War: Carthage strikes back.
218 BC	Romans defeated at Ticinus and Trebbia.
217 BC	Romans defeated at Lake Trasimene.
216 BC	Romans defeated at Cannae; Capua revolts; Roman navy raids Africa.
215 BC	Alliance of Carthage with Philip V of Macedon; Hanno enters Kroton; Roman navy raids Africa.

214–205 BC	First Macedonian War: Roman sideshow in Greece.
214 BC	Defection of Syracuse; Romans expel Carthaginians from Saguntum.
213 BC	Hannibal enters Tarentum; Romans besiege Syracuse.
212 BC	Romans besiege Capua.
211 BC	Hannibal marches on Rome (fails to prevent fall of Capua); fall of Syracuse (Rome recovers Sicily); Cornelli Scipiones defeated and killed in Iberia.
210 BC	Scipio appointed to Iberian command; Hannibal levels Herdonea; Roman navy raids Africa.
209 BC	Tarentum recovered; 12 Latin colonies refuse to supply troops; Scipio takes New Carthage.
208 BC	Scipio defeats Hasdrubal Barca at Baecula (Hasdrubal leaves Iberia); Roman navy raids Africa (Carthaginian fleet defeated off Clupea).
207 BC	Hasdrubal crosses Alps (defeated and killed at Metaurus); Roman navy raids Africa (Carthaginian fleet defeated off Utica).
206 BC	Scipio's victory at Ilipa (end of Carthaginian resistance in Iberia); Masinissa defects to Rome.
205 BC	Roman navy raids Africa; Mago Barca lands in northern Italy.
204 BC	Pact between Syphax and Carthage (marries Sophonisba); Scipio lands in Africa (begins siege of Utica); Masinissa joins Scipio.
203 BC	Burning of winter camps near Utica; Scipio's victory at Great Plains (Hannibal and Mago recalled); capture of Syphax (bittersweet death of Sophonisba); defeat of Mago (dies en route to Africa); Hannibal lands at Hadrumentum.
202 BC	Hannibal marches to Zama (Scipio and Hannibal meet); Scipio's victory at Zama.
201 BC	Carthage reduced to client status; Triumph of Scipio (takes cognomen 'Africanus').
200–197 BC	Second Macedonian War: Rome 'punishes' Philip V of Macedon.
200 BC	Philip lays siege to Athens.

198 BC	Philip retains Corinth.
197 BC	Philip defeated at Kynoskephalai; number of praetors raised to six (Hispania Citerior and Ulterior made Roman provinces).
196 BC	Hannibal elected *sufete* (political and economic reforms in Carthage); Rome proclaims Greek freedom.
195 BC	Hannibal flight and exile; Masinissa opens his raids on Carthaginian territory.
194 BC	Romans evacuate Greece; Hannibal in court of Antiochos III of Syria.
192–189 BC	Syrian War: Rome versus Antiochos.
191 BC	Antiochos defeated at Thermopylai.
190 BC	Seleukid fleet under Hannibal defeated by Rhodians; Antiochos defeated at Magnesia.
189 BC	Romans plunder Galatia.
188 BC	Peace of Apamea (division of Asia Minor between Pergamon and Rhodes).
186–183 BC	Pergamon–Bithynia War: Hannibal's last fight.
186 BC	Exile of Scipio Africanus.
185 BC	Death of Scipio Africanus.
183 BC	Death of Hannibal.
181–179 BC	First Celtiberian War.
181 BC	Revolts in Sardinia and Corsica.
176 BC	Final reduction of Sardinia.
173 BC	Envoys sent to arbitrate between Carthage and Masinissa.
172–168 BC	Third Macedonian War: Rome versus Perseus of Macedon.
168 BC	Perseus defeated at Pydna (end of Macedonian monarchy).
167 BC	Macedonia divided into four republics; Romans plunder Epeiros (150,000 people enslaved); Polybios taken to Rome.
163 BC	Final reduction of Corsica.
157 BC	Birth of Marius.

154–138 BC		Lusitanian War: a long 'small war'.
153–151 BC		Second Celtiberian War.
151 BC		Carthage declares war on Masinissa.
149–148 BC		Fourth Macedonian War: rising of the pretender Andriskos.
149–146 BC		Third Punic War: *Delenda Carthago*.
147–146 BC		Achaean War: end of Greek independence.
147 BC		Scipio Aemilianus takes command in Africa (tightens siege of Carthage); Macedonia made Roman province.
146 BC		Destruction of Carthage (Africa made Roman province); sack of Corinth; triumph of Scipio Aemilianus (takes cognomen 'Africanus').

THE CONSTITUTION OF CARTHAGE

Necklace pendants (Paris, musée du Louvre, AO 3783, 3784) of sand-core glass from Carthage, 4th or 3rd century BC, in the form of male human heads with beards. Such heads have been interpreted as a representation either direct or symbolic of the main deities, Tanit and Baal Hammon. The Phoenicians were celebrated in antiquity as glass makers, and the tradition continued in various centres of production in the Phoenician diaspora. (Fields-Carré Collection)

It is a truism that a state's political organization and military system go hand in hand. Before we look at the armies of Carthage, therefore, it is worth considering the constitution of Carthage. A governor, responsible to the king of Tyre, ruled Carthage at first; whether or not it had its own kings by the 7th century BC is far from clear. It is well known that Carthage is linked, in the foundation myth of the city, to the figure of a royal princess, Elishat (Timaios' Elissa, Virgil's Dido), yet Punic epigraphic sources always mention oligarchic-type magistracies as opposed to titles of a monarchical nature. However, in 574 BC a most far-reaching event took place when, after holding out for 13 years, Tyre lost its independence to the new superpower in the Levant, the Babylonians led by Nebuchadnezzar (r. 586–573 BC). The Phoenician colonies were on their own, and out of this uncertainty Carthage soon emerged as the leader.

At any rate, by the end of the 6th century BC the Carthaginian constitution had become decidedly oligarchic in nature. Thanks to the curiosity of Aristotle, who very much admired it as an example of what he labels a 'mixed form of government', we know something of the governmental system of the city during the period of our study. According to Aristotle, the 'mixed constitution', the ideal of Greek political theory and considered the natural condition for a civilized state, 'partakes of oligarchy and of monarchy and of democracy' (*Politics*, 1273a2). In Carthage it was headed by at first one, later two, annually elected chief magistrates called *sufetes* in Latin. Aside from their judicial role, they presided over the ruling council, convoked it and established the working agenda, and obviously resembled the consuls of Rome.

Nonetheless, unlike Rome, separately elected generals, invariably Carthaginian nobles, held the military commands in Carthage. This separation of civil and military powers was extremely unusual, if not unique, in the ancient world, but probably arose out of the very nature of Carthaginian armies. A body of 104 men, chosen from among the councillors in office and referred to as 'the hundred' by Aristotle (e.g. *Politics*, 1272b35, 1273a15), scrutinized the actions of these generals, and a commander who failed in the field had to explain himself. If the commander's explanation was not satisfactory, the punishment was often crucifixion *pour encourager les autres*. The epigram is Voltaire's (*Candide ou l'optimisme*, ch. XXIII), referring of course to the fate of the unfortunate Admiral John Byng, shot on his own quarterdeck after the sea battle off Minorca in 1757. Here we can compare the 'fate' of Caius Terentius Varro, the consul who fled from the field of Cannae in 216 BC. On arriving at the gates of Rome he was met by senators who publicly thanked him in front of a great crowd for not having despaired of the Republic. As the Roman Livy sagely remarks, a 'Carthaginian general in such circumstances would have been punished with the utmost rigour of the law' (22.61.14). The lucky Varro was then appointed to the command of a legion, while the unlucky survivors of the Cannae army, the common soldiers, were banished in utter disgrace.

Conversely, a too-successful Carthaginian general might suffer the same slow death, simply because 'the hundred' feared he might use his success (and hired army) to overturn the constitution, just as the general Bomilcar attempted to do in 308 BC with the backing of 500 citizens and 1,000 mercenaries (Diodoros, 20.44.1–6). Yet this draconian treatment of their commanders was accompanied

Modern bronze statue of Aristotle, Plateía Aristotélous, Thessalonika. Thanks to the curiosity of this Greek dialectician, we know something of the constitution of Carthage during the period of our study. In point of fact, this was the only non-Greek political system Aristotle dealt with in his treatise dealing with man as a political being and the nature of the state, the *Politics*. Interestingly, he knew of Rome too, but totally ignored that city. (Fields-Carré Collection)

Celtic iron swords of La Tène period. Blades were originally short (top), but improvements in iron technology resulted in the fearsome slashing sword (bottom). This was a blunt-ended longsword, which was wide, flat, straight and double-edged. Modern analysis of Celtic blades suggest they were very well made, with a good edge and great flexibility. (Ancient Art & Architecture)

by a freedom of action while in command, which did give a Carthaginian general a chance to gain valuable experience, something not given to a Roman general. We also hear that Carthaginian generals were held in high esteem (Justin, *Epitome*, 19.2.5), having obtained 'the honour of wearing as many armlets as they have served campaigns' (Aristotle, *Politics*, 1324b10).

It was largely through 'the hundred' that the ruling elite was successful in preventing the rise of tyranny through generals manipulating the mercenary armies that served Carthage so well. While military service was obligatory for native subjects, it was not so for native-born Carthaginians, whose numbers were too small to support a large, regular citizen army. Instead, warlike mercenaries, down to the time of the second war with Rome, were hired from

Énée racontant à Didon les malheurs de la ville de Troie, oil painting (1815) by Baron Pierre-Narcisse Guérin (1774–1833). This later poetic elaboration, made famous by Virgil, grandly ignores chronology and brings together Aeneas and Dido in a fiery relationship that ends tragically. For the Romans, however, the love of Dido for Aeneas serves the purpose of emphasizing Carthage's strange and alien culture, its otherness. (The Yorck Project)

various western Mediterranean peoples and, ever increasingly, from the Celtic lands in the north. It was the enormous wealth deriving from trade and tribute that made it possible for Carthage to employ mercenaries to fight on its behalf – a true privatization of warfare. By the 3rd century BC Carthaginians no longer served in Carthaginian armies, except of course as senior officers. The last occasion citizen soldiers served overseas had ended with their massacre at the hands of the Greeks on the banks of the Krimisos in Sicily in 341 BC. But that is to anticipate.

Last, but by no means least, there was a powerful executive body, what Roman writers called 'the senate' while the Greeks used various terms, including *gerousia*, a council of elders (e.g. Livy, 21.18.3 – senate; Aristotle, *Politics*, 1272b37; Diodoros, 20.59.1 – *gerousia*). It apparently had several hundred members, who probably held office for life, but whose method of appointment is uncertain. Nor is it clear what was the relationship between the 'senate' and the 'one hundred', though it usually assumed that the latter were members of the former. The powers of the citizens, however, were somewhat limited, the only real example of their political clout being the popular election of Hannibal Barca (Polybios, 3.13.4). According to Aristotle (*Politics*, 1273a7), if the *sufetes* and the senate were in agreement, they could decide whether or not to bring a matter before the people. Aristotle was writing when Carthage's power was at its height, and it is significant that some two centuries later Polybios says (6.56.3–8) that the power of the popular assembly grew over time.

Of course, our knowledge of the civilization of Carthage derives mainly from Graeco-Roman writers, who usually make use of a terminology that is peculiar to a Graeco-Roman institutional framework, and from the results of modern archaeological investigation. Still, in the objectively positive words of Cicero, 'Carthage would not have held an empire for six hundred years had it not been governed with wisdom and statecraft' (*de re publica*, 1 fr. 3). This is a fine tribute from a Roman at a time when the long and bitter struggle of the Punic wars was not yet a dim and distant memory. Also, as we shall discover in good time, some of the ancient world's finest soldiers came from the Punic family of Barca.

THE ARMIES OF CARTHAGE

At this point it is necessary to understand the basic composition of Carthaginian armies, without anticipating detailed discussion of weaponry and tactics. While the navy of Carthage was very much a citizen affair, as was to be expected from a maritime power with a permanent pool of trained sailors to fight in its naval wars, Carthaginian armies were generally of a mercenary character and tended to be raised for a particular conflict and disbanded at its end. It is most probable that, at least at the outset, the core of an army was made up of citizen soldiers, backed up by levies from tributary allies and a handful of foreign mercenaries who over time became the main component. Carthaginian coinage came to be widely distributed throughout Sicily in the first instance, and later throughout northern Africa and

'Phrygian' helmet (Karlsruhe, Badisches Landesmuseum, AG 245), so named because its shape resembled the 'Phrygian bonnet' worn during antiquity and borrowed during the French Revolution. The domed skull with lobate crown was normally made in one piece. This helmet pattern commonly had long, pointed cheek pieces. These were usually plain, but could occasionally extend to cover the whole face, leaving apertures only for the eyes and mouth and frequently decorated with embossed facial hair. (Fields-Carré Collection)

Sardinia, not only to check the economic power of the western Greeks but also to pay for those soldiers who were hired.

Citizen soldiers had been involved in the major events of the intermittent conflict against the Greeks of Sicily. A *corps d' elite*, which the Greeks described as a 'Sacred Band' (*hieròs lóchos*), was made up solely of native-born Carthaginians – resident aliens in Carthage did not qualify – and was held back in reserve during battles, moving into action only when there was a possibility of defeat. According to Plutarch (*Timoleon*, 29.4) this noble band of picked citizens was magnificently decked out in ostentatious armour. He talks too of 10,000 Carthaginian foot soldiers bearing white shields who fought in the war against the Corinthian Timoleon (*Timoleon*, 27.6). Here, we need to distinguish the citizens of Carthage itself from the Punic citizens of African and overseas cities. Diodoros, who in his history of his native Sicily is often at his best, says the Sacred Band consisted of 2,500 men, 'citizens who were distinguished for valour and reputation as well as for wealth' (16.80.4), so that the remaining 7,500 'Carthaginians' were probably ordinary Punic citizens. In this war the

CITIZEN CONSCRIPT, ZAMA 202 BC

It is a matter of some significance, perhaps, that it was not until after the tragedy of the Krimesos that native-born Carthaginians were conceived of primarily as a home guard to defend Carthage. From then on citizens were to be called to arms in times of national emergency, as they had been, along with the Sacred Band of Carthage, to defy the invasion force of Agathokles (Diodoros, 20.10.5–6), and would do so again a century later to confront the Roman invaders at Zama (Polybios, 15.11.2; Livy, 30.33.5).

Invariably, conscripts were pressed men with little stomach for the job, and a high proportion of them had never fought before. Polybios tells us that Hannibal's second line on the field of Zama consisted of Punic, Libyphoenician and Libyan levies hastily raised for the defence of Africa, and probably therefore with little preliminary training or previous experience. Apparently Hannibal looked upon these men as a cowardly lot, or so says Polybios (15.33.3), while in the soldier-historian's own considered judgement the Carthaginians made poor fighting material 'because they use armies of foreigners and mercenaries' (31.21.3, cf. Diodoros, 5.38.3).

Despite being a fresh-faced tyro, our young citizen of Carthage has equipped himself well. The great advantage of the Greek-style linen corselet (**1**) was its comfort, as it is more flexible and much cooler than bronze under an African sun. It is made up of many layers of linen glued together with a resin to form a stiff shirt, about 5mm thick. Below the waist it is cut into strips, *pteruges*, for ease of movement, with a second layer of *pteruges* being fixed behind the first, thereby covering the gaps between them and forming a kind of kilt that protects the wearer's groin. A linen corselet will not deflect glancing blows, but it will be as effective as bronze against any major thrust. To complete his body protection, he wears a 'Phrygian' helmet (**2**) with cheek pieces that cover all but his eyes and mouth. The cheek pieces themselves are superbly embossed with stylized curls to represent a beard and moustache.

The principal weapon of our citizen is a long thrusting spear (**3**). Fashioned out of polished ash wood and some 2.5m in length, his spear is equipped with an iron spearhead and bronze butt spike. As well as acting as a counterweight to the spearhead, the butt spike allows the spear to be planted in the ground when not in use (being bronze it did not rust), or to fight with if his spear snaps in the mêlée. In close-quarter combat the weapon is usually thrust overarm, the spear tip to the face of the foe, though it can be conveniently thrust underarm if charging into contact at a run. In both cases he will need to keep his elbows tucked close to the body in order not to expose the vulnerable armpit. The centre of the shaft is bound in cord for a secure grip.

Our citizen also carries a sword (**4**). This is the Greek *kopis*, a heavy, one-edged blade designed for slashing with an overhand stroke. The cutting edge is on the inside like a Gurkha *kukri*, while the broad back of the blade curves forward in such a way to weight the weapon towards its tip, making it 'point-heavy'. However, it is very much a secondary arm, to be used only when his spear has failed him. It is worn suspended from a long baldric from right shoulder to left hip, the scabbard being fashioned of wood covered with leather, with the tip strengthened by a small metal cap, the chape, usually moulded to the scabbard.

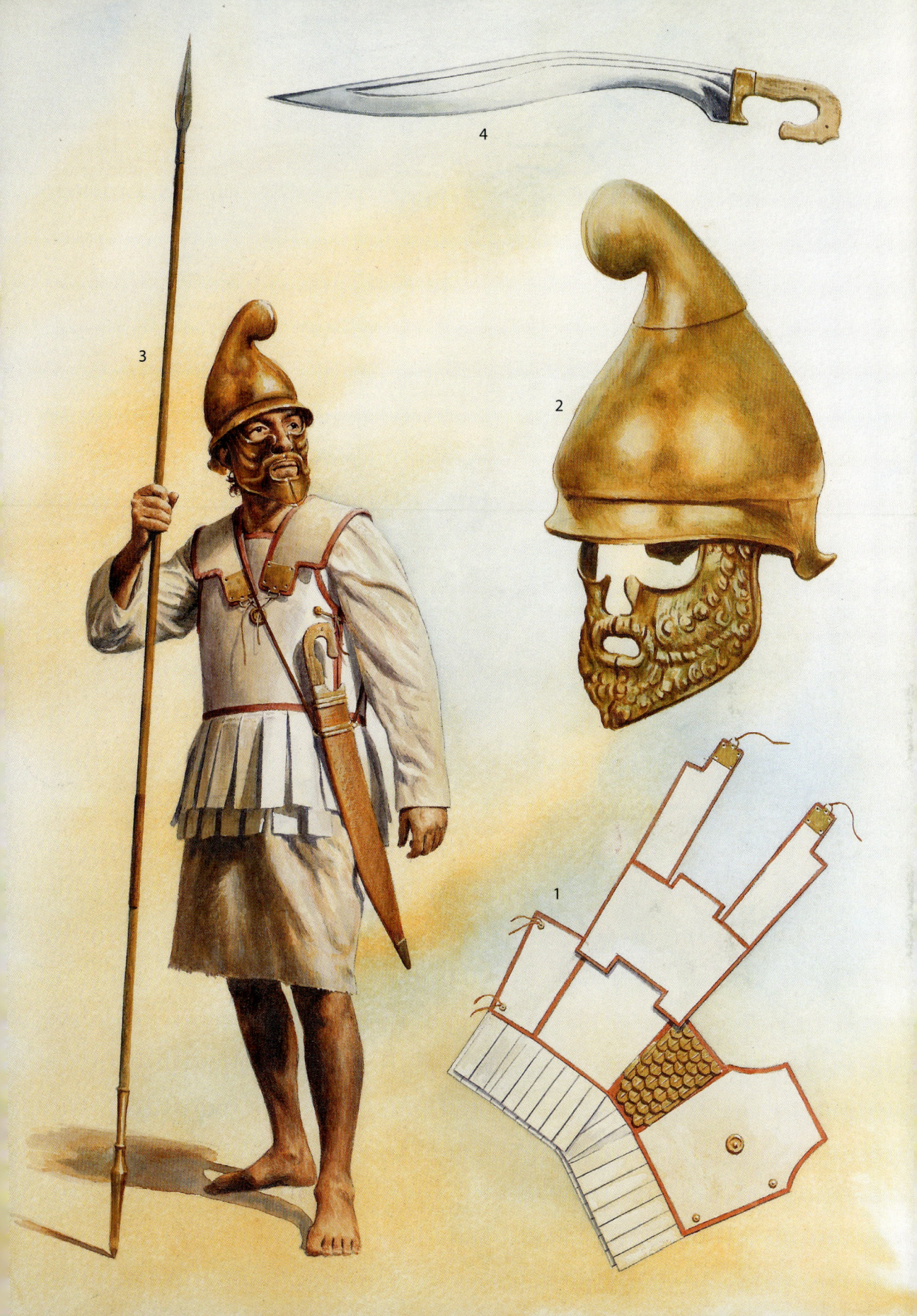

Sacred Band was destroyed utterly, and, after its second destruction three decades later, it appears no more in history.

Over the passage of time and according to the theatre of operations, Carthaginian armies became more and more heterogeneous as the deployment of Carthaginian citizens was gradually phased out in favour of subject levies and foreign mercenaries. We hear from Plutarch (*Timoleon*, 28.9) that Africa and Iberia were Carthage's great resource when it needed soldiers to fight its wars, the Carthaginians raising most of their levies from areas under Carthaginian rule, such as Africa, while mercenaries were hired from places with which Carthage had extensive trade links, such as the Balearic Islands or the Iberian peninsula. Thucydides (6.90.3), an experienced soldier, has his fellow Athenian general, Alcibiades, describe Iberian mercenaries as among the best fighters to be had in the western Mediterranean. Even so, Carthage's recruiting officers sometimes went much farther afield, scooping up mercenaries from overseas regions that were noted for the warlike character of their peoples, such as Gaul or Campania, or where training and discipline formed the basis of military prowess, such as the Greek world.

(A) Limestone relief (Madrid, Museo Arqueológico Nacional) from Osuna, Seville, depicting an Iberian warrior wearing a short linen or woollen tunic, usually white with crimson borders (e.g. Polybios, 3.114.4), and wielding a short but deadly sword, the *falcata*, a curved single-bladed weapon derived from the Greek *kopis*. (B) The blade was 35–55cm in length, though all we see here is the hilt, which is in the form of a horse's head that curves back to guard the knuckles. (C) He carries an oval body shield, much like the Italic *scutum*, hence the name *scutarus*. (Fields-Carré Collection)

By the time Carthage was raising armies for its wars with the Greeks in Sicily they were principally made up of subject levies and foreign mercenaries. The great army of Hamilcar (480 BC) was recruited from Italy and Liguria, Sardinia and Corsica, Gaul and Iberia and from the subject Libyans and Carthaginians themselves (Herodotos, 7.165; Diodoros, 11.1.5). The army of Hannibal (409 BC) had Carthaginians and Libyans too, stiffened by tough Campanian mercenaries who had formerly served Athens during its own ill-starred venture on the island (Diodoros, 13.44.1, 54.1). Three years later, when Hannibal was preparing his return to Sicily in greater strength, he sent his recruiting officers to Iberia, the Balearic Islands and to Italy for more Campanians, who were highly prized (Diodoros, 13.80.2–4). For his expedition against Syracuse (397 BC) Himilco hired mercenaries from Iberia (Diodoros, 14.55.4), while his successor, Mago (393 BC), commanded 'barbarians from Italy' as well as Libyans and Sardinians who were probably subject levies (Diodoros, 14.95.1). In the war against the Corinthian Timoleon (341 BC), the Carthaginians employed Iberians, Celts and Ligurians (Diodoros, 16.73.3). For the large army mustered to fight the war against Agathokles of Syracuse (311 BC), Carthaginian recruiting officers hired mercenaries from Etruria and the Balearic Islands, while the general himself, yet another Hamilcar, enrolled mercenaries in Sicily (Diodoros, 19.106.2, 5). The last we surmise to be Greeks since the army was later divided before Syracuse into two divisions, 'one composed of the barbarians and one of the Greek auxiliaries' (Diodoros, 20.29.6, cf. 31.1).

In point of fact, suffering a shock defeat in the early summer of 341 BC alerted Carthage to the excellence of Greek armoured spearmen, or hoplites, as soldiers. The disaster in question was the massacre on the muddy margins of the Krimisos, on the Punic side of Sicily, where even the crack Sacred Band was shattered and slaughtered by Timoleon's hoplite phalanx, the meat of which was made up of mercenaries (Parke, 1933: 173 n. 4). Post-Krimisos the Carthaginians, in the words of Plutarch, 'had come to admire them [hoplites] as the best and most irresistible fighters to be found anywhere' (*Timoleon*, 30.3), and, according to Diodoros, it was then that the Carthaginians decided to place their reliance more upon foreign soldiery and Greeks in particular, 'who, they thought, would answer the call in large numbers because of the high rate of pay and wealth of Carthage' (16.81.4). Sicilian Greeks had in fact served in Carthaginian armies previously, but as allies not as mercenaries (e.g. Diodoros, 13.54.6, 58.1). At the time, of course, the other main competitor in the Greek mercenary market was the great king of Persia. For, like Persia, it was hard currency that allowed Carthage not only to hire mercenaries in large numbers, but also allowed it the liberty to hire the best on the market. This, explains Diodoros, enabled the Carthaginians to win 'with their aid, many and great wars' (5.38.2).

Three decades later Carthage was to face, and survive, yet another crisis. When Agathokles landed in Africa, the Carthaginians, apart from those serving in the Sacred Band (Diodoros, 20.12.3, 7), put up only a feeble resistance to the invader, and orders for reinforcements were sent to Carthage's general in Sicily, Hamilcar. He shipped more than 5,000 men, and it is almost certain these were Greek mercenaries as we later hear of Greek cavalry in

Iron handgrip from a *caetra* from La Bastida de les Alcuses, Valencia. This sturdy example comes complete with the rings, also metallic, for a shoulder strap. When not in use, the *caetra* was suspended over the left shoulder by this long strap to hang on the back of the warrior behind his right arm. (Dorieo)

Africa, who were severely handled by Agathokles, and of 1,000 Greeks taken prisoner, of whom more than half were Syracusans, and presumably exiles from Syracuse (Diodoros, 20.16.9, 38.6, 39.4–5). Finally, many of Agathokles' soldiers, when he secretly sailed for home and abandoned them to their fate, made peace with Carthage and signed up to serve with the Carthaginians (Diodoros, 20.69.3).

One of the key lessons of the Krimisos for Carthage, though it is possibly more obvious to us in retrospect than it could have been to people at the time, was that it demonstrated the martial edge of the full-time hoplite mercenary over the part-time citizen soldier. Jason of Pherai was no man to argue with; he had the backing of 6,000 professional hoplites and he had personally trained his private army 'to the highest pitch of efficiency' (Xenophon, *Hellenika*, 6.4.28). The proof is in the pudding, as they say, for Jason now controlled his native land of Thessaly. Anyway, we shall pause for a moment and take note of our tyrant's views on the advantages of professionals over amateurs.

Citizen armies, Jason is quick to point out, include men who are already past their prime and others who are still immature. On top of this, few citizens actually bother keeping themselves physically in shape (Xenophon, *Hellenika*, 6.1.5). Jason's discipline was no doubt stricter than that of an elected citizen

IBERIAN LEVY, THE BAETIS 229 BC

Carthage had been employing mercenaries from the Iberian peninsula for a long time before its wars with Rome, but with the involvement there of the Barca family following the defeat in the first war many of the Iberian warriors serving thenceforth in Carthaginian armies did so as levies. They were nevertheless physically robust, brave and resourceful fighting men, regularly handling weapons and living a life of tribal warfare.

As those levied from tribal societies were taken from individual subsistence-level communities, and since the Carthaginians preferred not to homogenize their armies, allowing their troops instead to fight in their ethnic style, warriors like our Iberian here doubtless stood in the fighting line alongside close friends and family members. Small, closely related bands of warriors from kin groups would have contributed to a high level of *esprit de corps*, which in turn consolidated their fighting qualities, feelings of comradeship and friendly rivalry.

Generally, body armour seems to have been very rare and the combination of shield, sword, and short spear(s) or javelin(s) formed the equipment of most Iberian warriors. Here, Graeco-Roman authors make a clear distinction between two types: the *scutarus* (pl. *scutarii*) and the *caetratus* (pl. *caetrati*), the reference being to two types of shield. The first type carried a flat oval body shield, much like the Italic *scutum*, while the second carried a small round buckler, the *caetra*. Though a levy, nature at least had designed our Iberian for a *caetratus*. He is light, athletic and lissome, with a good length of arm.

The combination of sword and buckler, *caetra* and *falcata*, was apparently the most favoured war gear among Iberian warriors, and certainly would have been much more effective than the slashing sword of the Celt in a jammed situation, since the latter required not only a strong arm but room to swing the long weapon. The *caetra* (**1**) is made of hardwood, approximately 30cm in diameter, with metal fittings and ornaments on the face, and a large metal boss protecting a stout metal handgrip on the inside. Conveniently slung from a long carrying strap when not in use, in battle its lightness allows the warrior not only to parry enemy blows but also to punch with the boss or chop with the rim of the *caetra* too.

His other weapons are a bundle of javelins, each with a hard iron tip. Obviously this allows our *caetratus* to attack the enemy from a distance before closing in for hand-to-hand combat. To increase that distance, a javelin can be equipped with a finger loop (**2**), a thin leather thong that is wrapped around the shaft. Here we see the method of holding a javelin by a finger loop. The index finger and, usually, the second finger of his throwing hand would be inserted into this loop, while the two smallest fingers and thumb would lightly grip the javelin shaft. Javelins were made from a hardwood like cornel or a fine-grained elastic wood like yew.

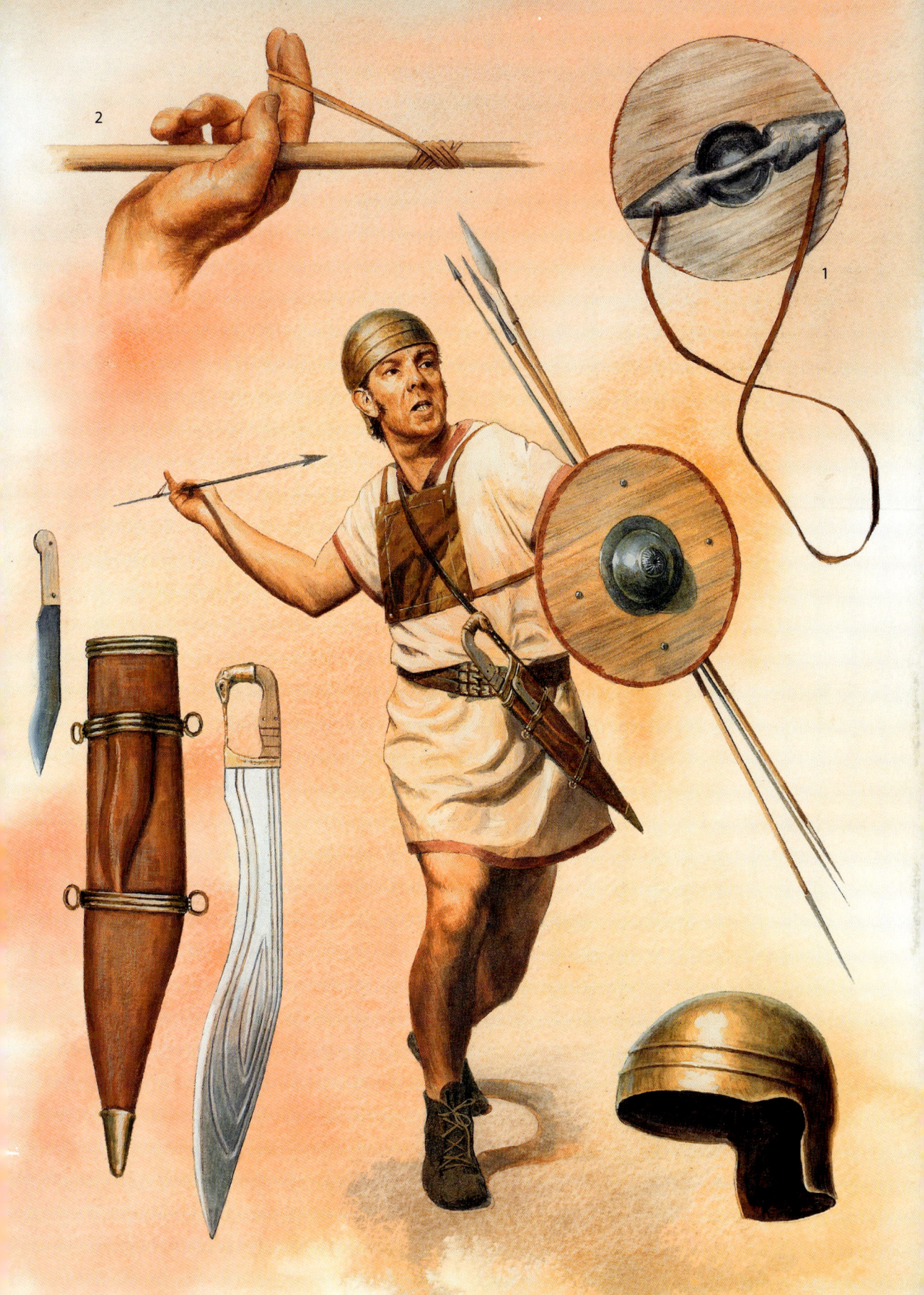

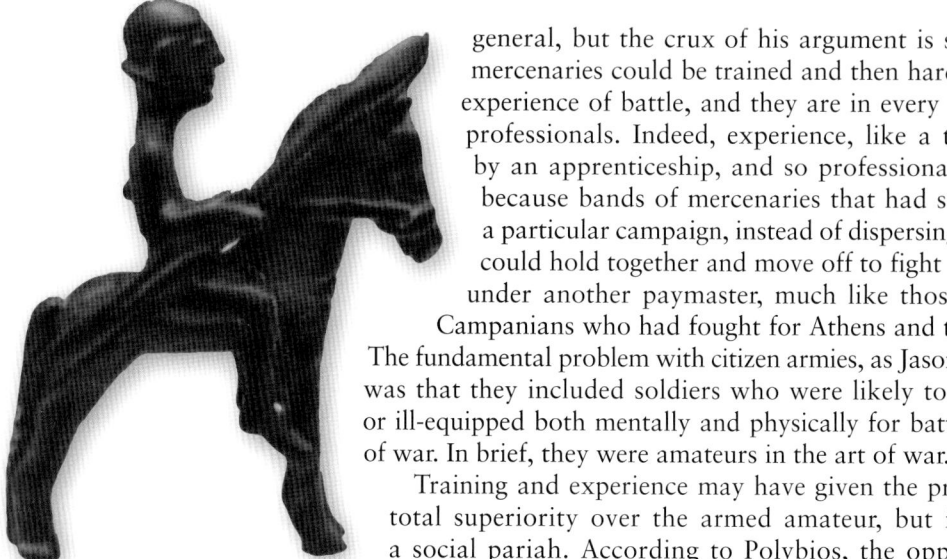

Bronze votary figurine (Madrid, Museo Arqueológico Nacional, 29323) from La Bastida de les Alcuses, Valencia. The horseman wears a close-fitting helmet and carries two javelins or short spears. Hanging on his back is a *caetra*, a small round buckler with a very substantial handgrip and a prominent boss, both metallic. Superb horse warriors, both the Carthaginians and Romans regularly employed contingents of Iberian horsemen. (Fields-Carré Collection)

general, but the crux of his argument is simple and direct: mercenaries could be trained and then hardened through the experience of battle, and they are in every sense of the word professionals. Indeed, experience, like a trade, was gained by an apprenticeship, and so professionalism was fostered because bands of mercenaries that had served together on a particular campaign, instead of dispersing at its conclusion, could hold together and move off to fight another campaign under another paymaster, much like those aforementioned Campanians who had fought for Athens and then for Carthage. The fundamental problem with citizen armies, as Jason fully appreciates, was that they included soldiers who were likely to be inexperienced or ill-equipped both mentally and physically for battle, the central act of war. In brief, they were amateurs in the art of war.

Training and experience may have given the professional soldier total superiority over the armed amateur, but it also made him a social pariah. According to Polybios, the opposing generals at Cannae stood up and made lengthy pre-battle speeches before their respective armies. The theme adopted by the consul, Lucius Aemilius Paullus, was that of obligation, namely that the citizen soldier fights not only for himself, but for his fatherland, family and friends too. Hannibal Barca, on the other hand, strikes a different chord and harangues his hired soldiery not on civic duty, but on the wealth to be gained through victory (Polybios, 3.109.6–7, 111.8-10, cf. 6.52.3-8, 11.28.7). Even if these two battle exhortations were rhetorical inventions of Polybios, they exemplify philosophic extremes: the dutiful and honest citizen soldier versus the greedy and anarchic hireling. The truth, as usual, lies somewhere in between and, besides, if there were a thousand reasons for being a soldier, patriotism would come far down the list.

Though they were a motley (if not mongrel) throng of mercenaries, treachery among the 'Noah's ark' armies of Carthage was rare. One example from the first war with Rome took place during the long and drawn-out siege of Lilybaeum, the most important Carthaginian base in Sicily. According to

Bronze figurine of a Gaulish warrior. Shields were normally flat boards of wood, and it is probable that they were usually faced with leather to protect them from the elements. Examples from La Tène stand 1.1m tall, but later depictions of warriors leaning on them suggest that in this period some were larger, perhaps 1.3m tall, like the contemporary Italic *scutum*. In shape they were often tall chopped ovals, or long rectangles with rounded ends, as here. (Ancient Art & Architecture)

Polybios, a group of mercenary captains, having talked things over, and convinced that the garrison would follow them, slipped out of the city at night to parley with the Roman commander. However, a Greek officer named Alexon, an Achaian, who had previously distinguished himself at the siege of Akragas, got wind of the treachery and informed the Carthaginian commander. Acting quickly, he assembled the remaining officers, and by means of lavish blandishments induced them to remain loyal to him. He then sent them to persuade their men to bide by their contracts. When the treacherous officers came up openly to the walls and endeavoured to persuade them to deliver up the city, they were driven off with a barrage of stones and missiles (Polybios, 1.43).

The other example from this long and weary war is the attempted betrayal of Eryx, the guerrilla base of Hamilcar Barca, to the Romans. The villains of this particular episode were a band of Gaulish mercenaries with an infamous career in robbery and treachery, which obviously fascinated Polybios (2.7.6–10). After having been driven out of their homeland by their compatriots, he says, these adventurers had been first employed by the Carthaginians as part of the garrison of Akragas, being then about 3,000 strong. This place they had pillaged as a result of a dispute over pay, perhaps early in the war, but presumably they had managed to break out with the rest of the mercenaries when the city fell to the Romans in 261 BC. Much later, as part of Hamilcar's command, around 1,000 of them tried to betray the town of Eryx, and when this ruse failed they deserted to the enemy, by whom they were put to guard the temple of Venus Erycina on the summit of the hill, where the Romans maintained a watchful garrison (242 BC). Inevitably, they also plundered that, and as soon as the war with Carthage was over, the Romans banished them from the whole of Italy. Still numbering about 800, they were then hired by the citizens of Phoinike in Epeiros, whom they then naturally betrayed too, to the Illyrian raiders of the autocratic Queen Teuta (230 BC). The remaining 2,000, under their war chieftain, Autaritos, returned to Africa and joined in the great mutiny of mercenaries (241 BC). Most of them were probably killed there in battle against their old commander, Hamilcar himself, though Autaritos escaped the destruction to be finally crucified with the other principal leaders (237 BC).

On the whole, the professional soldier was worth his salt until the first war with Rome was over, and he would, by the time of the next bout, supply the core of Carthaginian armies. Unlike a Roman army, therefore, a Carthaginian army was a heterogeneous assortment of races, and in the period of these two wars we hear of Libyans from subject communities, Numidians and Moors from the wild tribes of the northern African interior, Iberians, Celtiberians and Lustianians from the Iberian peninsula, deadeye shooters from the Balearic Islands, Celts or Gauls, Ligurians, Oscans and Greeks, a 'who's who' of ethnic fighting techniques. The army that Hannibal led against the Romans, for instance, differed more from Hellenistic and Roman armies, based as they were around heavily equipped infantry either in a phalanx or a legion, than the latter two did from each other.

As for the Libyan levies, which already made up one quarter of Carthage's army in 310 BC and which would be the foundation of the army Hannibal

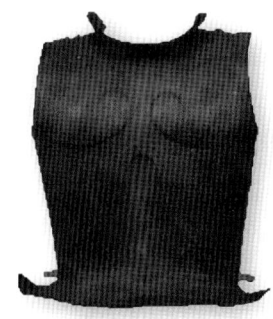

The shield carried by a hoplite was called the *aspis*. Built on a wooden core, it was faced with an extremely thin layer of stressed bronze and backed by a leather lining. Because of its great weight the shield was carried by an arrangement of two handles: an armband (*porpax*) in the centre, through which the forearm passed, and the handgrip (*antilabê*) at the rim. This is the bronze facing of an *aspis* (Olympia, Museum of Archaeology, B 4985) with the front plate of a bronze bell-shaped corselet (B 5101) recovered with it, from the 6th century BC. Note the size of the shield compared with the corselet. (Fields-Carré Collection)

brought to Italy (some 12,000 of his 20,000 infantry being Libyans) we cannot be entirely sure about these (Diodoros, 19.106.2; Polybios, 3.56.4). Ultimately the official status of the Libyans was probably largely irrelevant, as their true loyalty was neither to their half-forgotten families nor fatherland nor to the distant paymaster that was Carthage, but rather to their comrades and to their commander (Griffith, 1935: 232, cf. 219–20). Diodoros says that on Hamilcar Barca's death in Iberia, Hasdrubal the Splendid, his son-in-law, was 'acclaimed as general by the army and by the Carthaginians alike' (25.12.1). After Hasdrubal was murdered, so Polybios says, the soldiers unanimously acclaimed Hannibal as their general in spite of his youth, 'owing to the shrewdness and courage he had evinced in their service' (2.36.3). Later he picks up the story again, adding that the Carthaginians 'at first waited to discover how the army would respond, and when the news arrived that the soldiers had chosen Hannibal by universal acclaim as their general, they made haste to summon an assembly of people, which unanimously confirmed the soldiers' choice' (3.13.4).

Here may be seen a reflection of the fact that the Punic leadership in Iberia was a kind of personal absolutism vested in the Barca family, with a large degree of independence from the Punic establishment in distant Carthage, which accepted the fait accompli of the army's choice. Obviously the soldiers in Iberia were never motivated by loyalty to Carthage, the city that technically employed them, and simple greed was not enough to inspire them. Instead that ephemeral quality, *esprit de corps*, a soldier's confidence in himself and his army, developed, focusing on the mystique of the Barca family, while good fellowship bound them to one another. Hannibal's Libyans at Cannae were 'veteran troops of long training', says Frontinus, 'for hardly anything but a trained army, responsive to every direction, can carry out this sort of tactic'

RECRUITING BALEARIC SLINGERS, EBUSUS 206 BC

Balearic islanders, whose weapon par excellence was the sling, were clearly mercenaries; Polybios positively identifies them as such in his account of the Libyan War (1.67.7), and at Zama he firmly places them in the first line of Hannibal's army (15.11.1). Most in this line must have belonged to Mago's mercenary army, and presumably some of the Balearic slingers too, though they also may have included the 2,000 sent to Carthage by Mago in 206 BC (Livy, 28.37.9).

Historically, the mercenary soldier is either a member of a more militarily sophisticated society who sells his advanced skills to a more primitive army, or a member of a primitive society who sells his native-born ferocity to a more sophisticated army. Oftentimes, a mercenary's professionalism is exhibited by way of some specialized weapon alien to the military system that employs him. The Balearic slinger and his obvious skill with the sling is a prime example of this particular phenomenon.

Vegetius relates that the inhabitants of the Balearic Islands were 'said to have been the first to discover the use of slings and to have practiced with such expertise that mothers did not allow their small sons to touch any food unless they had hit it with a stone shot from a sling' (1.16). The author, possibly because of his national pride as an Iberian, adds a tinge of chauvinism to his description of the 'dead-eyed' islanders. The African Florus, on the other hand, simply says the 'boy receives no food from his mother except what he has struck down under her instruction' (1.43.5). Still, in the hands of an expert this herder's weapon was not to be underestimated.

The sling had always been the weapon of choice of the herder, who relied on its range and accuracy to keep predators at bay. However, life as a herder was hard and the living meagre. Here we see a band of hardy herders who have come down from their hills to offer their services as mercenaries. For Carthage their proficiency in long-range skirmishing made them a valuable component of its armies. Our slingers gather before a makeshift table set upon a beach, behind which sits a Carthaginian recruiting officer, a scarred veteran of many wars. He is protected by a well-armed bodyguard of tough-looking Libyans.

This 4th-century BC bronze statuette (Paris, musée du Louvre, Br 124) of a Samnite warrior is believed to have been found in Sicily, and thus possibly represents a mercenary serving there, perhaps in a Carthaginian army. He wears an Attic-type helmet with holes that once held feathers, a characteristic Oscan triple-disc cuirass, a broad Oscan belt and Graeco-Etruscan greaves. His shield and spear are missing. (Fields-Carré Collection)

(*Strategemata*, 2.3.7). He of course is referring to Hannibal's celebrated double envelopment. In other words, whatever they were before, subject levies or hired mercenaries, the Libyans were now professional soldiers serving in a private army.

RECRUITMENT

Whereas the call-up for Carthaginian citizens came at irregular intervals and probably affected only men above the age of 20, the levying of subject allies and the hiring of foreign mercenaries was a regular thing. Thanks to shoe-leather transport, delays caused by levies and the settling of mercenary contracts, getting an army together was a lengthy business. But the recruit thus had time to be conditioned by military society before facing the fear of wounds and the danger of death.

The levy was an unpopular method of recruiting warriors. When Agathokles landed in Africa, for instance, he received active support from the Libyans, who 'hated the Carthaginians with a special bitterness because of the weight of their overlordship' (Diodoros, 20.55.4). Similarly, Polybios writes that when the mercenaries mutinied against their masters, 'nearly all

Limestone relief from Osuna, Seville, depicting an Iberian warrior with a *caetra*. The *caetra*, from which this type of warrior takes his name (*caetratus*) was a round buckler with a prominent metal boss. It was held by a central handgrip, also metallic, and had a shoulder strap by which it could be slung on the back. Unusually, this warrior appears to be wearing some form of body armour, perhaps quilted fabric. (Fields-Carré Collection)

the Libyans had agreed to join in the revolt against Carthage and willingly contributed troops and supplies' (Polybios, 1.70.9). The mutineers had no difficulty in effecting a revolt of all the Libyan subject communities, who managed to put as many as 70,000 men into the field (Polybios, 1.73.3). As well as their menfolk, these communities, in the cause of their freedom, willingly donated their money, which more than made up the sum owed to the mercenaries by Carthage (Polybios, 1.72.5–6).

When it came to the actual business of levying, it seemed Carthage laid down some sort of quota on the basis of tribal population figures. The Oretani and the Carpetani were on the verge of rebellion in 218 BC, seizing and retaining the recruiting officers because of the severe demands that Hannibal put upon them (Livy, 21.11.13). In order to retain the loyalty of individual tribes to Carthage, he granted leave of absence, following the capture of Saguntum, to any Iberian warriors who wished to visit their families before setting out to Italy in the springtime (Polybios, 3.33.5; Livy, 21.21.5–8). Meanwhile, Iberian recruits were stationed in Africa, acting both as garrisons and hostages, and thousands of others were allowed to return home prior to the crossing of the Pyrenees. Some 3,000 Carpetani, according to Livy, having already deserted (Polybios, 3.33.7–11, 35.6–7; Livy, 21.21.10–13, 23.4–6). It was not Carthaginian policy to allow levies to stay in their home areas.

We now turn from the levy to the mercenary. By and large two types of mercenary recruiting were (and still are) common. It was carried out either by recruiting officers or directly through diplomatic channels and interstate treaties that included clauses allowing citizens to serve as soldiers for an agreed wage for the contracting parties. The last was a tried-and-tested method, as a state or ruler that needed mercenaries would procure them through a friendly power that controlled a source of supply. This arrangement can be seen in operation when Carthage recruited Numidians from friendly princes. Those on the coast came under the influence of

D **THE MUTINEERS MAKE THEIR DEMANDS, LIBYAN WAR 240 BC**

Mercenary soldiers were generally better trained and motivated than citizen soldiers, with consequently better tactical flexibility, and they had more experience and were less prone to panic. Despised by moralists and tolerated by governments, in times of war they were invaluable. However, mercenaries could be difficult to control, especially when faced with the prospect of easy gain. And when governments could dole out nothing to mercenaries, they sickened, deserted or turned on their officers or, worse, on their employer. Their purpose, however, was not revolution but retribution.

In this reconstruction, Hanno 'the Great' has arrived to investigate the cause of the mutiny. The celebrated Carthaginian general is the conqueror of Hekatompylos (Diodoros, 24.10; Polybios, 1.73.1), the farthest point Punic conquest will ever reach – it is some 160km south-west of Carthage – and its subjugation marked the culmination of some years of savage 'small wars' against local tribes, as Polybios hints when he says Hanno was 'accustomed to fighting with Numidians and Libyans' (1.74.7). He was apparently the 'generalissimo' in Africa, and judging by what Polybios says about his extortions from the Libyans, had been for some years (1.67.1, 72.3). Today he stands on a makeshift timber platform whilst the mutineers crowd around and gaze sullenly at this man Carthage has sent to speak to them. Timidity never pays. The great lesson of military history is that a single daring stroke can save a forlorn situation.

As is fitting for his exalted position, Hanno is gorgeously dressed in his finest robes, bears a sword, and his left arm is adorned with golden armlets – these signify the number of campaigns in which he has fought. He is bareheaded, but shaded by a parasol carried by his black African attendant. The latter wears wristbands and large earrings, all of copper. In the background cluster the solemn Carthaginian officers.

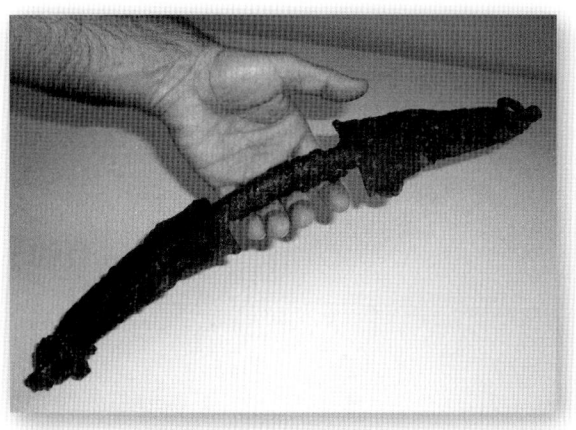

Iron handgrip from a *caetra*, provenance unknown. The Iberian round buckler known as the *caetra* could be anything between 30 and 45cm in diameter, and was equipped with a circular metal boss that protected a centrally placed handgrip. Gripped in the fist, which was positioned directly behind the boss, its size made it poor protection against missile weapons but extremely handy at deflecting the blows from bladed weapons. (Pguerin)

Carthage and it is known that the princes of Numidia were allies of the Carthaginians at one time or another, and presumably their famed horsemen were, in theory at least, allies rather than mercenaries. In the war with the renegade mercenaries the Carthaginians were greatly helped by a friendly Numidian prince, Naravas, who offered to defect with his followers, and eventually fought for them with 2,000 horsemen. He was awarded by marriage to the daughter of a man he much admired, none other than Hamilcar Barca (Polybios, 1.78.1–11).

When recruiting was not backed by diplomacy, the usual practice was to dispatch recruiting officers to localities from which mercenaries were to be found or raised. Thus, as we have already discussed, the Carthaginians sent their recruiting officers far and wide, to the peninsulas of Iberia and Italy, the islands of Sicily and Sardinia, the lands of the Celts, and so on, with large sums of money to make the preliminary payments. During the First Punic War, Carthage cast its net wider and sent recruiting officers to Greece, who returned with plenty of mercenaries and the brilliant *condottiere* Xanthippos, 'a man who had been brought up in the Spartan discipline, and had had a fair amount of military experience' (Polybios, 1.32.1). It does not seem likely that Carthage can have had previous agreements with Greek states, but the recruiting officers obviously knew where to go in order to find military job hunters.

Plainly, such men needed an intimate knowledge of the current mercenary market and, as such, doubtless included the entrepreneurial mercenary captain who first petitions and then negotiates the contract with the employer, and subsequently recruits and leads the men to fulfil it. We have already mentioned the disturbances within besieged Lilybaeum, and the mercenary captains 'called a meeting of the soldiery and partly by entreating them, partly moreover by assuring them that each man would receive the bounty the general had offered, easily persuaded them to bide by their engagements' (Polybios, 1.43.5). As to the actual mechanics of the recruiting process, however, we have very little evidence. From medieval Italy, on the other hand, comes the term we are all familiar with, *condottieri*, which originated from the contracts of employment, *condotte*, between a mercenary captain and his employer. Such contracts were very detailed, originally of a short-term nature but by the 15th century usually ran for periods of six months to a year.

Finally, there were the casual methods of recruiting mercenaries. The most obvious of these methods was that of winning over mercenaries currently in the pay of the enemy. The term 'mercenary' was (and is) often used in pejorative descriptions. Confusion is often apparent in discussions when the term is used, and it usually has more to say about the writer's political bias than it does about the man described. As discussed before, a true mercenary is a professional soldier whose behaviour is dictated not by his membership of a socio-political community, but his desire for personal gain. He should not discriminate between causes and states to which he offers his services, the acid test being whether he would switch sides for more money.

Desertions and surrender on the part of the mercenaries were but excuses for their keeping a weather eye to the main chance, as 200 of Agathokles' mercenaries did when they went over to Carthage (Diodoros, 20.34.7). Another good example of infidelity on the part of mercenaries, again Greek, was the occasion when Timoleon lost no less than a quarter of those that he had employed through fear of the size of the opposing Carthaginian host (Plutarch, *Timoleon*, 25.3). But such unscrupulous behaviour was not peculiar to the Greeks. There were the Celtic contingents who left the service of Rome and entered that of Carthage, butchering and decapitating some of their erstwhile allies as they did so (Polybios, 3.67.1–4), or the Numidian and Iberian horsemen who went over to the Romans after Hannibal suffered a reverse (Livy, 23.46.6), or the Iberians who left the service of Carthage and entered that of Rome after the fall of their garrison (Livy, 24.47.8–9).

These last two examples were, as far as we know, the only occasions when Hannibal lost men through desertion during the time he was in Italy. As Lazenby (1978: 106) points out, these two desertions were a sign of the times, the virtual deadlock in Italy offering few chances of booty for Hannibal's men. Livy writes that meanwhile, in another theatre of war, the Romans had obtained the services of the Celtiberians 'at the same rate of pay as had been previously offered by the Carthaginians' (Livy, 24.49.8). The two Cornelii Scipiones are reputed to have employed 20,000 of these Celtiberians (the number probably much exaggerated), and it was their desertion, through Carthaginian bribery, which caused the defeat and death of Cnaeus Cornelius Scipio (Livy, 25.32–34 *passim*). What the hired soldiers of these armies had in mind was not to fight to the death, but to be on the winning side, to profit, and above all to survive. In an age of mercenary armies the rules were simple: when X beat Y the mercenaries of Y became the mercenaries of X.

EQUIPMENT AND APPEARANCE

The clothes worn, the weapons wielded, and the burdens carried by those that served in the armies of Carthage, soldier or warrior, amateur or professional, were generally similar to those of other peoples of the ancient world, but obviously exhibited some regional and ethnic variations. Oscan clothing, for example, was very similar to that worn by an Iberian warrior, being little more than lightweight buskin boots and a short sturdy tunic frequently covered by a woollen cloak. The same can be said of their accoutrements of war,

One of the commonest designs throughout the Italian peninsula, the Montefortino helmet offered good defence from downward blows. It was basically a hemispherical bowl beaten to shape, with a narrow peaked neck-guard and an integral lead-filled knob for a crest. Large cheek pieces protected the face without obscuring the wearer's vision or hearing, and those of this 3rd-century BC Samnite example (Karlsruhe, Badisches Landesmuseum, AG 197) are identical in design to the Oscan triple-disc cuirass. (Fields-Carré Collection)

ABOVE

'Thracian' helmet (Corfu, Museum of Archaeology), a style bafflingly named because it apparently evolved from a Thracian cap. The cheek pieces of this particular helmet pattern were fully developed, extending below the chin to provide some protection to the throat, while the eyes and nose were shielded by a metal brim. This fine example, high-domed and low-crested, is silvered. (Fields-Carré Collection)

ABOVE RIGHT

Front plate of a bronze muscled cuirass (London, British Museum, GR 1842.7.28.712) from southern Italy, dated to c.320 BC. Originally connected to a back plate by a system of pins and hinges and ties at the shoulders, its *pteruges* are also missing. Sculptures of the period show three sets of *pteruges* protruding from the bottom of the cuirass, rather than the two sets as were common in the previous century. (Fields-Carré Collection).

and throughout our chosen period the main ones in use were the spear, the sword, the dagger, the javelin, the sling and the bow. The first three were used in the close-quarter mêlée, and the rest were missile weapons. All weapons had their particular advantages. The bow was more effective at a distance than the javelin, and the spear reached farther than the sword.

Protection for the body in the form of armour or helmets seems to have been a rarity amongst warriors, usually restricted to nobles. Obviously no one who went to war would feel entirely safe without some form of head protection, and no one would pass up the chance of grabbing one if he possibly could, whatever was handed down to him by his father or taken from the dead – friend or foe. To give a feeling of security, simple conical caps of *cuir bouilli* were used at the very least, and anything that would protect the head from the blows of the enemy could have been pressed into service. Each man would bring whatever he could afford or could scrounge on an individual basis.

For the most part, however, the only things that prevented a combatant's death or serious injury in the hurly-burly of battle were his own martial prowess, his physical strength and agility and his shield. This was by far the cheapest and commonest item of war gear, and it was the most useful item in battle too. Rich or poor, young or old, no warrior could afford to be without a shield. It was the main line of defence against all forms of attack, and if used skilfully it could make helmets and body armour well-nigh redundant.

Spear

Of all the weapons man has invented, the spear is the one most universally used during this period, and in a very real sense it was the weapon of the ordinary freeman. Whereas the sword was a weapon of military and political elites, the spear was pretty much a common workaday weapon.

Iron corselet (Thessalonika, Museum of Archaeology) from the Royal Tombs of Vergina, which apparently once belonged to Philip II of Macedon. It actually consists of iron plates (5mm thick), four for the body and two for the shoulders, and is decorated with narrow gold bands and six gold lion heads. The *pteruges* no longer survive. The iron was covered on the inside with plain cloth and on the outside with decorative cloth, making it resemble a *linothorax*. The tomb also produced an iron helmet. Interestingly, the members of the Sacred Band, according to Plutarch, enjoyed 'the protection of their iron corselets and helmets' (*Timoleon*, 28.1). (Fields-Carré Collection)

In its simplest form, a spear is nothing more than a wooden stick with a sharpened and hardened end. Ash was the most frequently chosen because it naturally grows straight and is capable of withstanding a good hard knock without splintering. However, some fruit woods, such as the cornelian cherry, have good qualities. In order to be able to sustain some lateral damage in use, shafts had to be around 22mm in diameter.

As the main arm for most warriors, the spear, unlike the javelin, was usually employed as a far-reaching stabbing weapon and as such it would rarely have left its owner's hand on the field of battle. Spearheads came in a range of shapes and sizes, and with socket ferrules either closed and welded or split. In our period the most common designs were angular blades, with a diamond cross section, and leaf-shaped blades that were normally lenticular in section. The addition of a midrib gave greater longitudinal strength to a spearhead, increasing its effectiveness at piercing shields and armour during hand-to-hand spear play.

Vachères warrior (Musée municipal de Vachères), 1st century BC, showing the characteristic mail shirt of interlocking rings, a heavy woollen cloak, tubular torc and sword belt of the aristocratic Celtic warrior. A long slashing sword, for all to see, hangs at his right hip and he leans on his shield in characteristic Gaulish fashion. The sword was usually suspended from a bronze or iron chain around the waist, which passed through a loop at the back of the scabbard. (Fields-Carré Collection)

It is difficult to say with any certainty what the best length for a spear was, but common sense dictates that it would have been generally around 2–3m long. Any shorter and the chief advantage of keeping the enemy a whole pace away is gone; any longer and it becomes awkward and too wobbly to use accurately with one hand. Of course, it also had to be light enough to wield one-handedly (usually overarm) and used in conjunction with a shield. Finally, apart from the obvious use of being able to dispatch a foe beyond arms' reach, the spear has the significant advantage that it used a minimum amount of expensive bronze or iron in its construction.

Splendid triple-disc cuirass (Tunis, musée de Bardo) from a tomb at Ksour-es-Sad, Tunisia, complete with the hinged straps that passed under the arms and over the shoulders. This was probably taken back to Africa by one of Hannibal's veterans, perhaps an Oscan-speaking warrior who fought (and survived) in the third line at Zama. A characteristic broad, bronze belt, the symbol of manhood, would accompany this armour. (Fields-Carré Collection)

Iberian warriors used two types of sword, the curved and the straight. The first type, known as a *falcata*, was a variant of the Greek *kopis*. Here we see an example of the second type, a straight sword (and dagger) from Almedinilla, Córdoba, 4th or 3rd cnetury BC. The relatively short blade was sharpened on both edges and had a long, tapered stabbing point. Housed in a framed scabbard, it was suspended from a waist belt using a stable ring suspension system, which, like the sword type itself, was later copied by the Romans. (Fields-Carré Collection)

Sword

Most of the fighting that took place in contemporary battles was at close quarters. When it came to swordplay there were two fundamental ways of striking an opponent: the first was the thrust, a stabbing motion using a straight sword, and the second was the cut, a slashing motion using a curved sword. The thrust usually inflicted mortal wounds while even multiple slashing cuts were seldom fatal. Just as Vegetius rightly points out, 'A cut, whatever its force seldom kills, because both armour and bones protect the vitals. But

a stab driven a couple of inches is fatal; for necessarily whatever goes in penetrates the vitals' (1.12). A sword, used in conjunction with a shield, could be devastating at the point of contact when in the hands of a trained swordsman.

The Iberians used a relatively short but deadly sword. This was either the *falcata*, a curved single-bladed weapon derived from the Greek *kopis*, or the cut-and-thrust sword, which was a straight-bladed, sharp-pointed weapon from which the Roman *gladius* was derived. Of the last, Polybios says that 'the point of the Iberian sword was no less effective for wounding than the edge, whereas the Gaulish sword was useful only for slashing and required a wide sweep for that purpose' (3.114.2, cf. 33.5; Livy 22.46.6).

Polybios describes (2.33.3) how some Celtic swords were of poor metal, so much so that they bent on impact, thereby requiring the owner to retire and stamp the blade back into shape with his foot before re-entering the fray. This view is contradicted by the archaeological record, which suggests Celtic swords were very well made with a good edge and great flexibility. Polybios' story of swords that bend reads

ABOVE
'Dying Gaul' (Rome, Musei Capitolini, MC 747), Roman copy of the 2nd-century BC Pergamene original. The Celts had a fearsome reputation for aggressiveness, even among the militaristic Romans, and there can be no doubt that initially they were terrified by these bigger-than-life warriors, who adorned themselves with gold torques, wore long moustaches and had hair that was slaked with lime to make it stand up like a horse's mane. (Fields-Carré Collection)

RIGHT
Limestone relief (Madrid, Museo Arqueológico Nacional) from Osuna, Seville, depicting an Iberian warrior wearing greaves and, perhaps, body armour of a quilted nature (see photograph on p.27). Beneath him is a fallen warrior wearing a belted tunic and carrying a *caetra*. The *caetrati* were obviously 'sword-and-buckler men' trained (and equipped) to fight in a close formation with sword and shield. (Fields-Carré Collection)

LEFT
Life-size replicas of Gaulish garments and war gear (Paris, musée de l' armée, 16). Iberian warriors, armed as they were with a relatively short sword, required little space to perform their swordplay, resulting in a much tighter tactical formation. Celts, on the other hand, required a fair amount of room to swing their long slashing swords effectively, the blade of which could be up to 90cm in length. (Gorinin)

BELOW
Straight dagger from the necropolis of La Osera, Ávila, 4th or 3rd century BC. This weapon nicely reminds us that Iberian straight swords and daggers were the forbears of the *gladius* and *pugio*, the characteristic trademarks of the Roman legionary for some four centuries. This fine example, richly inlaid with silver, has an 'atrophied antennae' pommel. That is, the iron hilt has been drawn up into two 'horns' terminating in ball-shaped ornaments. This is a characteristic feature of Iberian straight-bladed weapons. (José-Manuel Benito)

Dagger and scabbard frame with three suspension rings (Madrid, Museo Arqueológico Nacional), from the necropolis of La Osera, Ávila, from the 4th or 3rd century BC. The ring suspension arrangement, which we normally associate with the Romans, was essentially Iberian in origin. Housed in scabbards, they were hung from a belt using a ring suspension system, which was also copied by the Romans. This clever system allowed a warrior to draw either of his blades quickly in combat without exposing either his left or right arm. By inverting the hand to grasp the hilt and pushing the pommel forward he drew the weapon with ease, an asset in a close-quarters situation. (Fields-Carré Collection)

like one of those tall tales told by soldiers to while away idle moments around the campfire. Nevertheless, other authors took up Polybios' comments and criticisms. The one notable exception is Philon of Byzantium (*fl. c.*200 BC) who, in an illuminating passage written around the time of Polybios' birth, describes how the Celts test the excellence of their swords:

They grasp the hilt in the right hand and the end of the blade in the left: then, laying it horizontally on their heads, they pull down at each end until they [the ends] touch their shoulders. Next, they let go sharply, removing both hands. When released, it straightens itself out again and so resumes its original shape, without retaining a suspicion of a bend. Though they repeat this frequently, the swords remain straight. (Philon, *Mechanike syntaxis*, 4 (= *Belopoiika*) 71)

Swords exhibited various general and local fashions during the La Tène period. Blades were short from the 5th to the 3rd centuries BC. Unlike bronze, iron was worked by forging rather than casting. Improvements in iron technology, along with changes in fighting style, resulted in the two-edged sword designed for slashing, often of enormous length and round-ended, in the 2nd and 1st centuries BC. Surviving examples of this period have an overall length of about 85–90cm, with some having a blade length of 90cm without the hilt. Quality varies, but few of these blades descend to the poor quality described by Polybios, indeed, many are carefully balanced for maximum effect as slashing implements.

In the hands of a tall Celtic warrior with a long reach the weapon could be a deadly blade and made him, especially amongst shorter opposition with shorter swords, the most respected of foes. The main requirement for using the long slashing sword was muscular strength, as the warrior twirled his weapon high in an attempt to slash the shoulder or neck of his opponent with hefty sword blows. Its blade would have inflicted horrific injuries, particularly on the left side an opponent's head and upper body, but its use would have caused fatigue pretty quickly.

Obviously not contrived for finesse, nonetheless the sword was considered the weapon of choice for the high-status warrior, and to carry one was to display a symbol of rank and prestige. Perhaps surprisingly it was worn on the right, hanging from a sword-belt of metal chain that rested on the hips. The chain passed through a suspension loop on the back of the scabbard and kept the weapon upright, helping to prevent the sword from becoming entangled with the warrior's legs as he walked or ran. In fact, it was fairly easy to draw even a long blade from this position.

Dagger
For close-quarter work if all else failed, or for delivering the *coup de grâce* to one's fallen enemy, the favoured weapon was the dagger. So whatever other weapon soldiers or warriors carried, a spear, a sword, a javelin, and so on, they usually had this handy extra blade tucked away somewhere about their person.

Normally, the blade of this shock weapon was short, with two sharp edges and a sharp point. It was designed primarily for stabbing, rather than slashing, to penetrate deep into the body of an opponent – though creating only a narrow wound. Of course, a dagger was also useful for those more mundane chores in the field, and was commonly regarded as a tool as well as a personal weapon.

The earliest daggers were made from a single sheet of flat metal, while later examples were made with a clearly defined midrib to the blade, which gave additional strength to the cutting edges. Handles were of wood, bone or ivory, and scabbards of wood or leather were used to protect the blades when not in use. These early examples were small enough to be carried tucked into the belt of a warrior's tunic. Otherwise, they could be carried on a band around the arm. The arm dagger is a weapon habitually worn by peoples of Saharan and Sudanic Africa, amongst them the Tuareg, a branch of the fair-skinned Berber race. The style here was to keep it in a sheath attached to the inner side of the left forearm by a loop, the sheath and loop usually of leather but sometimes of metal, such as decoratively engraved brass. The blade points to the elbow and the hilt rests against the inside of the wrist, from which position it can be quickly drawn (Spring, 1993: 30, 43).

A *soliferreum*, a slender all-iron javelin used throughout Iberia. It has a small barbed head and, though not seen here, tapers to a point at the butt. Most examples vary in length between 1.6 and 2.0m. The *soliferreum* was a very effective short-range missile, where the concentration of its ample weight in the small head enabled it to punch through shield, armour, flesh and bone. (Dorieo)

Javelin

The javelin, unlike the spear, was designed for throwing. Weighing less than 1kg, it was light enough to hurl a considerable distance, and the devastating effect of a javelin thrown at close quarters should not be underestimated. It need not have been razor-sharp to be effective. Its relatively thin shaft was nonetheless incapable of sustaining lateral damage.

Javelins, particularly those in the hands of warriors or professionals, could be equipped with a finger loop: a thin leather thong, 30–45cm in length, which was wound round the middle of the shaft near the centre of gravity, leaving a loop of 7–10cm for the index and, usually, the second finger of the throwing hand. The loop provided leverage and acted like a sling to propel the javelin, and as it was launched the thong unwound, having the same effect as the rifling inside a rifle barrel; it spun the javelin, ensuring a steadier flight. The loop was never tied to the shaft of the javelin, but was merely wrapped

Surviving leaden sling bullets are typically about 35mm long and about 20mm wide, and weigh approximately 28g. These acorn-shaped examples (Mozia, Museo G. Whitaker, M 3207) probably belong to the time of Dionysios' siege of Motya. These leaden bullets, the most effective of slingshots, could be cast, and often bore inscriptions, such as symbols or a short phrase, usually of only a few letters. Whereas slingshots are common finds, slings themselves are exceptionally rare. (Fields-Carré Collection)

round and came free after the throw. Experiments sponsored by Napoleon III suggest that, after sufficient practice, a javelineer might more than double the distance of his throw.

Javelins were common throughout northern Africa and Iberia, though what the Greek authors called the *saunion* was a distinctive Iberian weapon,

E — XANTHIPPOS ADDRESSES THE TROOPS, TUNIS 255 BC

Ancient battles were dramas without an audience, and when the moment of battle approaches, when the lives of men under him, the issue of the combat, even the fate of a campaign (not to mention a country) may depend upon his decision at a given moment, what happens inside the heart and vitals of a commander?

Some are made bold by the moment, some indecisive, some clearly judicious, some paralysed and powerless to act. Soldiers respect a commander who is competent. They admire a commander who is competent and bold. When he is an accomplished student of war, leads boldly, and also savours gambling his own life, he acquires a certain mystique. He is a soldier's soldier. Cautious commanders will shake their heads at this love of danger and condemn it as daredevilry, which it often is. They secretly admire it, however, and wish they had as much faith in their luck and power to lead lesser men that the mystique confers.

The Spartan Xanthippos was clearly a man of parts who lived by his wits, that much is clear to us, but it would be nice to know if he managed to survive and thus was able to die in his bed. Having reached the top of the profession, it was Xanthippos who saved Carthage from the Romans, and then vanished suddenly and (maybe) for ever. Carthage owed everything to this mysterious Spartan, and Polybios does not fail to give his fellow Greek his due, considering him a striking vindication of Euripides' sagacity that 'one wise counsel conquers many hands' (1.35.4). In the very hour of his triumph Xanthippos disappears from the scene, quitting Carthaginian service, possibly for that of Egypt. Tunis was to prove Carthage's only victory in a land battle during the first war with Rome.

Fighting spirit is the mood a good commander strives most earnestly to generate and sustain in his army. Naturally, proper concern for his men's welfare by provision of regular rations, prompt pay and creature comforts – the 'sinews of war' – is one means to achieve it. Exhortation is another; a commander can appeal to the pride and loyalty of his men, or manipulate them through promises of lasting fame and material rewards. Whether or not a commander addressed his entire army en masse, particularly one with linguistic diversity, is a debatable point. Anyway, Xanthippos' eve-of-combat harangue takes the form of a simple pep talk as he slowly walks along the line of battle. In this way he addresses the men in a few brief but well-chosen words, his encouraging apophthegms shouted back to those beyond earshot.

Xanthippos is wearing a *pilos* helmet adorned with a fore-and-aft horsehair crest. This style of helmet derives from a felt conical cap actually called the *pilos*, which was possibly first worn as a protection underneath closed helmets (such as the Corinthian helmet, which completely encased the head) and later translated into bronze. The *pilos* helmet is light and provides all-round vision, and seems to have first been adopted by the Spartans . The helmet terminates in a discernable point, very much like a sugarloaf, and has a narrow rim that does not stick out at all but follows the line of the crown, hanging almost vertically from the body of the helmet.

As of old, Spartan hair continues to be carefully dressed (and oiled) in four locks falling to the front, two on either shoulder, and four to the back. Likewise, the upper lip continues to be shaved while the beard is generally kept long. Spartan tradition has it that long hair makes a fine-looking man more handsome, and an ugly man more frightening.

Originally a garment typically worn by labourers to allow free movement of the right arm, the Spartans wear the *exomis* for warfare. This woollen tunic is two-sleeved, but the right-hand sleeve can be let down to leave the right shoulder and arm free to handle weapons in combat (providing, of course, the warrior lacked body armour). However, over his *exomis* Xanthippos wears a silvered cuirass richly decorated in relief.

Despite the rather ornate armour, Xanthippos wears the trademark Spartan cloak. Called a *tribôn*, it is habitually described as 'mean', that is to say, thin as opposed to short. Spartan boys under training had to wear the same cloak in summer and winter in order to become accustomed to the cold. Self-denial is the keynote of the Spartan lifestyle, and warriors would visually emphasize their toughness by making use of a single woollen cloak in rain or shine, allowed to wear thin and never washed. Like the tunic, it is dyed crimson.

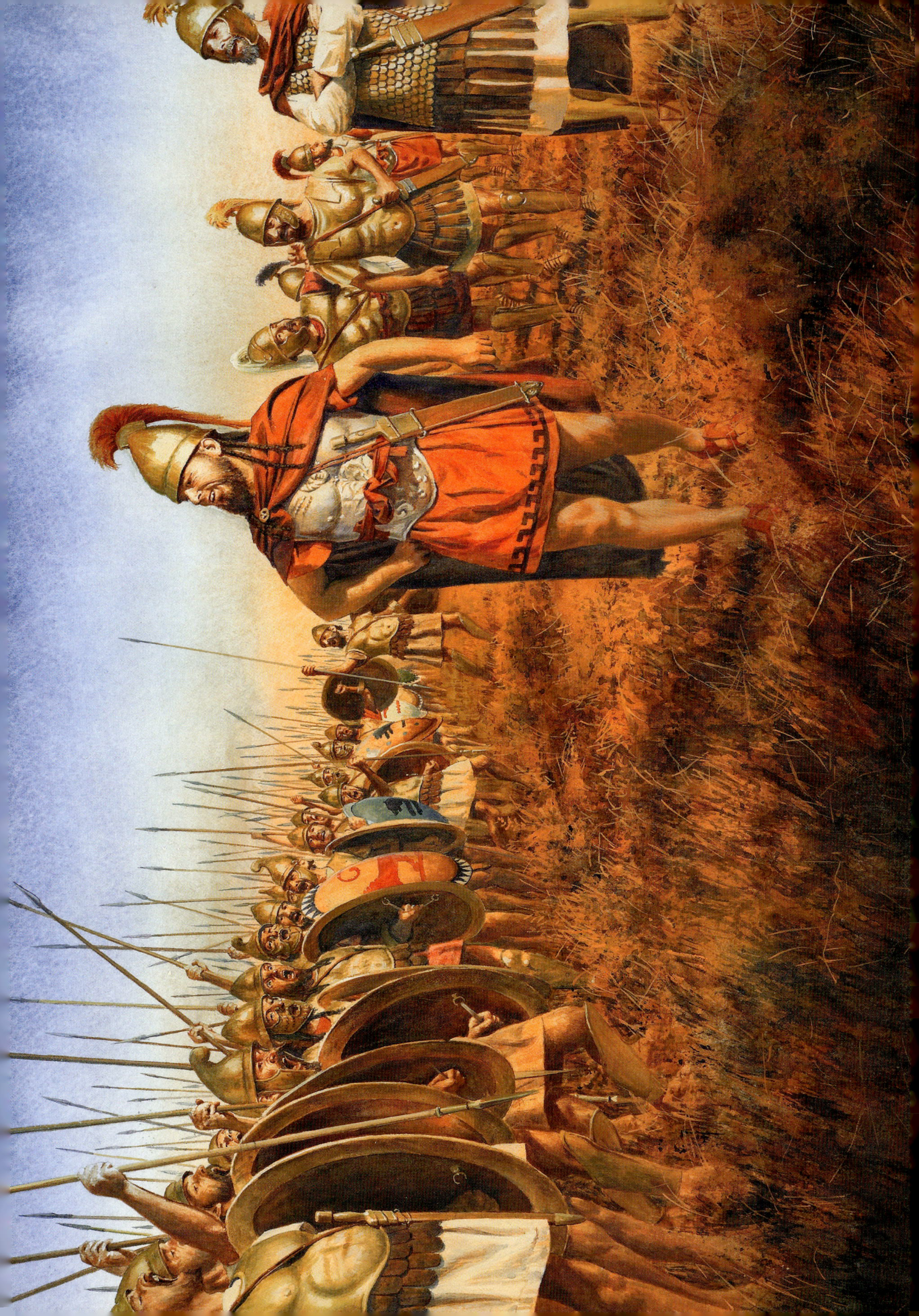

Long before Carthage and Rome, of course, specialists in the use of sling and stone were a regular feature of the armies of the ancient world, particularly in the Near East. Whilst such a fighting style might seem biblical to us moderns, a high degree of skill and marksmanship was required, and once mastered the results could be horribly deadly. This is a decorative carving depicting the duel between David and Goliath, from the west façade of the Armenian Cathedral of the Holy Cross (AD 915–21), Akhtamar Island, Lake Van, Turkey. (Lostinafrica)

a slim javelin, about 1.6–2m long, made entirely from iron (Latin *soliferreum*), with a small barbed weapon head and a pointed butt. According to Strabo (5.4.12) it could punch through helmet, shield or body armour, and then embed itself in flesh or bone. Another type had an iron shaft tipped with a barbed weapon head, around 20–30cm long, riveted to a wooden shaft. It was thus similar to the Roman *pilum*, and may have served as a model for it.

Sling

Since the time of David the sling had been popular with herdsmen to protect their charges from predators, since ammunition was readily to hand in hill country (ideally round stones or pebbles), and thence it came to be used in battle. Slingers normally served as a complement to archers, the sling not only out-ranging the bow but a slinger was also capable of carrying a larger supply of ammunition than an archer. Slingshots were not only round stones or pebbles, but also of lead, acorn or almond shaped, and usually weighing some 20–30g, but occasionally up to 55g. Onasander makes it clear that it was essential for slingers to have room to use their weapons, as they needed 'to execute the whirling of their slings' (*Stratêgikos*, 17). This whirling action obviously built up speed before one end of the sling was released, projecting the bullet, and modern experiments with slings have demonstrated that they can have an effective range of 200m or thereabouts.

The sling, as deadly as it was simple, was made of inelastic material such as woven reeds, rush, flax, hemp or wool. It comprised a small cradle or pouch to house the bullet, and two braided cords, one of which was secured to the throwing hand and the other held, simultaneously, between the thumb and forefinger of the same hand. After a single whirl around the head it was then cast, the bullet being fired at the moment that the second cord was released, its range being related to the angle of discharge, the length of the whirling cords and the amount of kinetic energy imparted by the thrower. A fast-moving slingshot could not be seen in flight and did not need to penetrate armour to be horrifically effective (Onasander, *Stratêgikos*, 19.3; Arrian, *Ars Tactica*, 15.2). A blow from a bullet on a helmet, for instance, could be

Attic red-figure stamnos (London, British Museum, GR 1843.11-3.1) attributed to the Achilles Painter (c.450–c.440 BC). The scene shows an Athenian hoplite departing for battle. His panoply includes a *linothorax*, bronze greaves and a 'Thracian' helmet, of which several styles were common in the 4th century BC. Such accoutrements would also have been worn by members of the Carthaginian Sacred Band at the Krimisos, though their spears were much shorter. (Fields-Carré Collection)

enough to give the wearer concussion, if not a more serious injury (Celsus, *De medicina*, 5.26, 7.55).

We know that Balearic slingers normally carried extra slings, and that those not in use were normally tied round the head or the belly (Strabo, 3.5.1; Diodoros, 5.18.3; Florus, *Epitome*, 1.43.5). Unlike their Rhodian counterparts from the other end of the Mediterranean, they did not use lead bullets as slingshots, preferring stone instead. Ammunition was carried in a bag slung over the shoulder. It is assumed that slingers also carried a sidearm, such as a dagger or even a sword, and perhaps even a buckler, such as the Iberian *caetra*.

Iron boss from a *caetra*, from the necropolis of El Cuarto, Griegos, from the 5th or 4th century BC. A bowl-shaped protrusion, with a diameter of 33.5cm and a thickness of 2mm, this boss gave ample room for the shield hand. The *caetra* was used in conjunction with the *falcata*, and *caetrati* were renowned for their ability (and agility) in this type of 'sword-and-buckler' combat. Obviously in combat the *caetra* was not only effective at parrying blows, but was an extremely useful secondary weapon, the *caetratus* using the hefty boss to punch his opponent. (Luis García)

ON CAMPAIGN

Employers of mercenaries had a reluctance or inability to disgorge pay. In the six months during which Xenophon and his fellow Greek mercenaries, known in history as simply the Ten Thousand, served Cyrus the Younger, he paid them only once, and even then only after they had protested vigorously (Xenophon, *Anabasis*, 1.2.11–12). It seems that the Persians had the infuriating habit of being 'mean and niggardly' (Anon., *Hellenika Oxyrhynchia*, 19.2) when it came to paying their mercenaries. Such underhand behaviour, however, could easily cause serious repercussions for the employer. After the war with Sparta, for example, Aratos was unable to recruit mercenaries because the Achaian League had not paid their mercenaries in full during that conflict (Polybios, 4.60.2). Then again, the following year, old grievances appeared to have been forgotten and the League was able to recruit with some success. The mercenaries soon disbanded, however, when their pay fell into arrears (Polybios, 5.30.5–6). The almost chronic inability of employers to produce pay on time, or at all, also meant that from those who did not desert because of it there was constantly the threat of mutinies. It was a case of '*Point d' argent, point de Suisse*' (Racine, *Les Plaideurs*, I.i.15).

Salary and sustenance

The Libyan War arose out of a difficulty over pay, and this unhappy event throws a valuable spotlight upon the ways and means by which mercenaries were, in theory at any rate, maintained. Carthage had not paid its hired soldiers by the month or any other regular interval, but in the course of the First Punic War had run up a rather generous slate with the mercenaries in Sicily, who must now be evacuated from the island in accordance with the terms of the peace treaty with Rome. Moreover, there was no choice but to ship them to Africa, there to receive their considerable arrears of pay and collect their baggage and families. It seems that the standard procedure was to recruit mercenaries in their respective homelands and then concentrate them in Carthage before proceeding to the theatre of operations (Polybios, 1.66.3, 7).

In his good account of the events of the mercenaries' mutiny, Polybios does not fully inform us about their sustenance. Clearly, during the years of continuous warfare in Sicily, they must have received regular rations in some form or other. For the time spent in Africa waiting for their pay to be prepared, they each received 'a gold stater for pressing expenses' (Polybios,

F — OSCAN MERCENARY, ZAMA 202 BC

Often, campaigning mercenaries had families to return to, provided of course that they made the return trip. Our authorities minimize losses in battle and say almost nothing of losses from sickness, though bacteria must have carried off far more men than blades. Anyway, though worn with travel and fighting, his face thin and drawn by privation, our Oscan mercenary has survived the wars and returned home. He is one of Hannibal's veterans, who fought and survived at Zama. The battle itself, which turned out to be the last of the Hannibalic War, must have been a grim business, since, as Polybios points out (15.14.6), the antagonists were equal in spirit and courage.

Our returning mercenary is depicted in a short linen tunic and an Oscan belt (**1**). This is a broad leather belt, some 10cm in breadth and covered with bronze sheeting, fastened with two elaborate hooks and beautifully embossed. Accentuating the waist and drawing attention to the groin area (see photograph on p.26), it is the very symbol of the wearer's manhood.

One of the commonest designs throughout the Italian peninsula, the Montefortino helmet (**2**) offers the wearer good protection from downward blows. Moreover, large cheek pieces protect the face without obscuring the wearer's vision or hearing and, fittingly, those of this Oscan example are identical in design to the triple-disc cuirass. Our mercenary also wears a pair of bronze greaves, Greek-style (**3**).

Prominent, however, is his splendid bronze body armour (**4**), the triple-disc cuirass peculiar to an Oscan warrior. This consists of three symmetrical bronze discs placed on the chest and the back. Our fine example is based upon that found in a tomb at Ksour-es-Sad, Tunisia, which has the lower disc replaced with a bust of a goddess adorned with a triple-crested helmet. She is probably Athena Promachos, Champion Athena, a very appropriate patron for a professional warrior.

Our mercenary also carries a body shield (**5**), the Italic *scutum*. A shield of this type was discovered at Kasr-el-Harit in Fayûm, Egypt (Connolly, 1998: 132). It is midway between a rectangle and an oval in shape, and is 1.28m in length and 63.5cm in width with a slight concavity. It is constructed from three layers of birch laths, each layer laid at right angles to the next, and originally covered with lambswool felt. This was likely fitted damp in one piece, which, when dry, shrunk and strengthened the whole artefact. The shield board is thicker in the centre and flexible at the edges, making it very resilient to blows, and the top and bottom edges may have been reinforced with bronze or iron edging to prevent splitting. Nailed to the front and running vertically from top to bottom is a wooden spine.

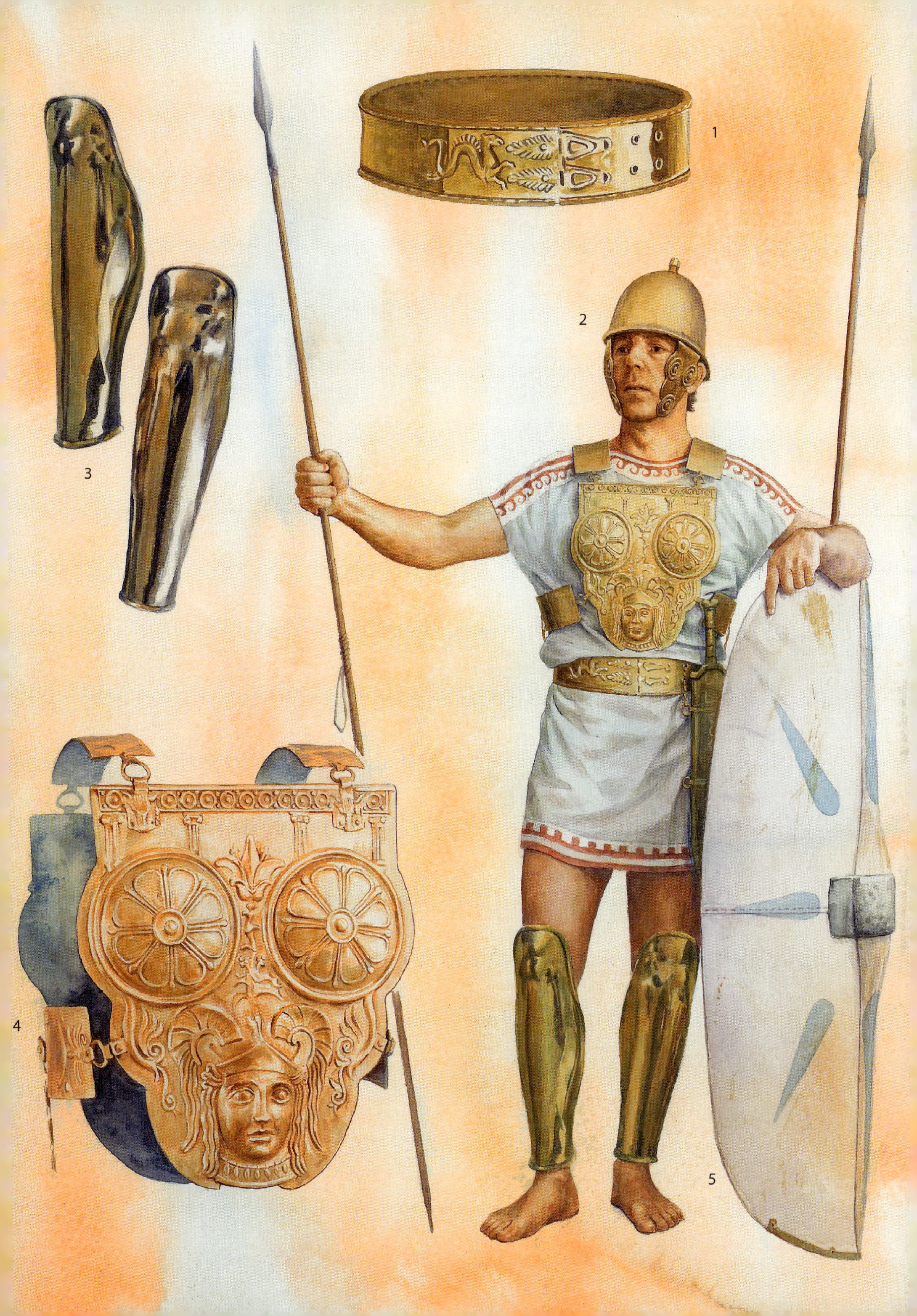
1
2
3
4
5

1.66.6). Equivalent to the remuneration for a month's labour, the object of the payment was of course to enable the soldiers to buy their food for themselves. For the authorities then provided a market, and in their eagerness to be accommodating, allowed the soldiers to fix their own prices for the commodities they needed (Polybios 1.68.5).

Such a measure was obviously a reflection of the fact that local markets dealing with soldiers had a nasty habit of bumping up the prices and, occasionally, the soldiers would retaliate by taking matters into their own hands. Because they needed civilians for the bare necessaries of life, soldiers were open to exploitation by them, welcomed merely as chickens ripe for the plucking. On the other hand, because civilians needed the profit derived from filling a soldier's belly, slaking his thirst and satisfying his lusts, they were exposed to his unruly behaviour. 'But how come you so bare?' the peace-loving intellect Erasmus once asked the soldier of fortune. 'Why', he replied, 'whatsoever I got from pay, plunder, sacrilege, rapine and theft was spent in wine, whores and gaming' ('The soldier and the Carthusian', *Colloquies*, 1518, vol. 1). As the mercenary-poet Archilochos, in his typical earthy way, sang: 'Long the time, hard the work that went into heaping the wealth, he threw away on whores' (fr. 142, cf. fr. 72). Though exaggerated for effect, this merely colours common knowledge.

The standard rate of pay for a soldier in the Mediterranean world during the 3rd century BC varied greatly over time and place, but generally it included his daily rations plus money in wages, though the former could be commuted in kind for cash and thus the recipient received composite pay (namely salary plus sustenance in cash). A soldier's wages were reckoned from the first of each month and paid at the end of that month, or even, perhaps, each year, while his rations, as we shall see shortly, were evaluated at a specific amount of cereal per day (e.g. Austin 95, Burstein 55, Sage 293). Yearly contracts of employment were usually for nine or ten months, and the soldiers were expected to support themselves during the two or three months of idleness, but as mercenary pay was a heavy drain on the treasuries of states arrears were frequent.

Of course war might bring death, disease, or a dearth of pay, but there was always the hope of a windfall. Pay, when received, did not represent much wealth, and a soldier believed he was entitled to pick up a little extra when and where he could. It is said hope is a cupbearer to war and, in all probability, the quick road to wealth for the mercenary was by plunder, especially after victory upon the field of battle where there were spoils to be garnered: equipment and the contents of purses and baggage trains. After a successful siege there was always looting, even though this was conventionally permitted only if the defenders had refused to surrender in its initial stages. It was certainly through looting that mercenaries made up any shortfalls in their wages; a complete explanation in itself of all the destruction wrought by such troops. But for all its prospects, and here that fool's-gold glint of plunder continued the age-long romantic notion of something for nothing, the profession was generally unremunerative. It was adopted by men, oftentimes escaping from under-caloried privation, for want of a better occupation to provide them, as they hoped, with a regular source of income and food.

Pay may well be less than generous and all too often in arrears, but an army, said Napoleon, or so we are reliably informed, marches on its stomach. There are no truer words in the annals of military affairs than these. How to feed and water the men (and their animals) was probably the most important initial requirement on campaign, and one which found its way down to the

We should remember that, as in almost every era of human history as late as the American Civil War, any battle represented a golden opportunity for the survivors to re-equip themselves at the expense of the fallen – friend or foe. A large amount of war gear, as well as money and trinkets, would normally change ownership during the lull after combat. Though much later in date, this 1st-century BC relief of Roman legionaries could easily represent Hannibal's Libyans at Cannae. (Ancient Art & Architecture)

Reconstruction of Gaulish arms and armour. Here we see the characteristic long slashing sword of the Gaulish warrior, designed to deliver powerful over-the-shoulder blows. It was certainly not contrived for finesse, or even to cut someone into ribbons, but a weapon designed to either hack an opponent to pieces or to beat him to a bloody pulp. (Fields-Carré Collection)

humblest command. It was a constant in every military plan, and remains so to this day.

As previously mentioned, in the 3rd century BC a professional soldier's rations were issued as a measured amount of cereal. Herodotos (7.187.2), in his account of Xerxes' invasion of Greece, reckons the Persian troops were receiving a daily ration of one *choinix* (1.08kg) of cereal per man. It was the Roman practice in the 2nd century BC, according to the contemporary testimony of Polybios (6.39.13), to issue a monthly ration of cereal equal to two-thirds of an Attic *medimnos* (34.56kg) to each legionary, which is more or less equivalent to the daily allowance of the one *choinix* Xerxes' campaigning soldiers were receiving some three centuries before. In a similar yet comic vein, Aristophanes suggests, 'for one giant loaf, use just one *choinix*' (*Lysistrata*, 1207), which was regarded as a slave's ration by well-fed stay-at-home aristocrats (Athenaios, 6.272b). Just by way of a comparison, the chain gang of Cato ate 4–5 Roman pounds (1.31–1.64kg) of bread per day, but they consumed little else. All in all, the evidence safely allows us to assume that the basic daily diet of a soldier in our period of study would have consisted of one *choinix* of cereal, more or less.

One cereal or another has formed the staple basis of the human diet in every corner of the world since agriculture first began. In the ancient Mediterranean world barley and wheat were the two main grains – oats, popular among Celtic and Germanic tribes, were viewed as a weed and thus considered fit only for animals, while rye, the closest relative of wheat, was a 'northern' grain. Barley was generally known as 'fodder for slaves' (Athenaios, 7.304b) and considered far less nourishing than wheat, so much so that by the 4th century BC the preference for wheat and the bread made from it, in moneyed circles at least, had ousted barley from its prominent position in the Mediterranean diet. Thus, wheat became the 'corn' or staple cereal in the Mediterranean basin, and barley the cheaper but lowly alternative. Thus in the Bible we read 'a *choinix* of wheat for a denarius, and three *choinikes* of barley for a denarius' (Revelations 6:6), the measure of wheat being sufficient for a man for one day at a price equivalent to a labourer's daily wage. Finally, in the Roman army, so Polybios tells us (6.38.2), soldiers were fed on barley instead of wheat as a form of punishment.

Although barley could be turned into various dishes, such as gruel or soup, it was normally eaten as a type of baked unleavened dough. Barley, unlike wheat, is normally husked and cannot be freed from its cover-glumes by ordinary threshing and is, therefore, roasted or parched prior to use. Unfortunately, this process destroys the gluten content of the grain – this determines the baking qualities of flour – thereby making it unsuitable for leavened bread. Still, as yeast was yet to make its debut, 'bread' in this period was really unleavened crust and would have looked somewhat like modern pitta and is an ancestor of the pizza.

For Archilochos the spear not only brought death and suffering but also provided the run-of-the-mill vocational soldier with his daily bread (fr. 2). In fact, the mercenary-poet is fairly specific and describes his bread as a 'kneaded thing of barley' (Greek *mâza*). Made for the occasion, Archilochos' bread had been made of barley grain that had been milled to produce barley meal, and soldiers (or their soldier-servants if they could afford to maintain one) had to convert their daily ration of grain into meal themselves. Thus querns were to be found amongst the mundane equipment necessary for an army simply because they were, as Xenophon explains, 'the least heavy amongst implements used for grinding grain' (*Kyropaideia*, 6.2.31). This meant that the soldiers could carry unground grain and thus reduce the risk of spoilage, as well as allowing them to take advantage of ripe grain collected on the march, just as Hannibal's men did in the vicinity of Gerunium (Polybios, 3.100.6). Most soldiers, if not all, were accustomed to seeing the daily supply of grain being ground out by hand on a quern at home.

Having roasted and milled his barley grain, the soldier took his meal and kneaded it up with a little oil and wine, using a square of sheepskin as a kneading-trough, to produce a simple form of bread (e.g. Hermippos, fr. 57, Kock). The fresh dough was rolled into wafer-thin strips and then baked quickly. The soldier would usually do this by twisting a strip around a stick and baking it the hot ashes of his campfire. It would have been consumed

Oscan belt from Italy, late 5th or early 4th century BC. Here we see the metal furnishing only, the leather having long perished. The two large clasps are rather ornate, tapering into elongated arrowheads that curl around at their points. Riveted attachment plates shaped like palmettes are used to attach these clasps to the belt. Manufactured from a hammered sheet of bronze, this was then stitched to a leather lining by means of small drilled holes, which are clearly visible along both the top and bottom edges. (Claire H.)

Painted plate (Rome, Museo Nazionale di Villa Giulia) from Capena, Campania, showing a war elephant and calf. Unmistakably an Indian elephant, and possibly one of those brought to Italy by Pyrrhos of Epeiros, Florus describes (*Epitome*, 1.13.12) how a cow-elephant, anxious for her offspring's safety, spread havoc among Pyrrhos' army. This breed was large enough to carry a wooden howdah, the one here suggesting light slat over a heavier frame, and equipped with a large round shield hung outside (on each side presumably) for additional protection. (Fields-Carré Collection)

hot, otherwise, being unleavened, it would have gone rock-hard. The quality of the bread itself tended to be poor; indeed, it would have contained substantial traces of abrasive minerals (feldspar, mica, sandstone, etc.), introduced into the flour as it was laboriously ground on the coarse stone of a quern. Over a period of time this grit wore down the enamel of teeth, causing at best some discomfort and pain, and at worst, serious abscesses and infections, which could prove fatal.

Despite Xenophon's claim (*Kyropaideia*, 1.2.11) that when he was truly famished even barley bread tasted sweet, the ex-mercenary elsewhere implies (*Anabasis*, 2.4.28, 4.4.9, 7.1.37) that it was usually helped down with a little

Hannibal in Italy, fresco (1503–08) attributed to the Bolognaise painter, Jacopo Ripandi (*fl. c.*1500–*c.*1516), in the Palazzo dei Conservatori, Rome. Looking very much like a gentleman from the Orient, Hannibal rides an elephant. It is said that when he crossed the great morass that was the Arno Valley, the general himself rode his last surviving elephant, an animal that may be identified as the Indian elephant Cato called Surus. (Fields-Carré Collection)

local wine and a wedge of cheese, with beans, onions, garlic and olives as likely accompaniments. Unfortunately, the paucity of evidence does not allow us to say much for those who served Carthage. Plato says (*Laws*, 674a4) that the imbibing of alcohol was banned in its armies. Polybios, on the other hand, points out that the mutineers were bibulous beyond belief after their accustomed breakfast (1.69.11), while at the Metaurus many of the Gaulish mercenaries apparently slept during the encounter inebriated – in the aftermath of the battle they were to be butchered in their beds 'like sacrificial victims' (11.3.1). Elsewhere he informs us that Hannibal's soldiers, on the morning of the battle of the Trebbia, were rubbing themselves down with

Rating himself as third after Alexander and Pyrrhos, Hannibal was overly modest. His victories were certainly more impressive than those of Pyrrhos, and his strategic focus was clearer. Although Alexander achieved spectacular conquests, he did so using the superb Macedonian army created by his father, whereas Hannibal achieved his successes with an ad hoc collection of polyglot mercenaries. This is a marble statue of Hannibal (Paris, musée du Louvre) by Sébastien Slodtz and François Girardon, dated between 1687 and 1704. (Fields-Carré Collection)

olive oil while taking breakfast around their campfires (3.71.6). So we know that wine and olive oil were part of their daily ration, but other than that and vague references to 'corn/grain', 'abundant provisions/supplies' or 'foraging expeditions/parties' (e.g. 3.49.11, 51.12, 68.8, 69.2, 90.3, 7, 92, 100.2, 7, etc.), Polybios takes it as a matter of course and does not anticipate our ignorance.

One principle does, however, emerge as a consistent rule of thumb throughout our period: the ancient Mediterranean world was largely a cereal-eating culture, deriving its proteins from pulses and dairy produce from sheep or goats. This picture had some variants. Mountain people lacked the olive, while those that dwelt by the sea had access to its particular fruits. Nonetheless, we can safely assume that a campaigning soldier lived mainly on those ubiquitous staple commodities: bread, cheese and wine.

Cheese made from sheep's or goat's milk contains fewer calories but more protein than an equivalent weight of bread. Onions, garlic and olives contain considerably less, pulses contain a similar amount of calories but more protein and olive oil contains many more calories but no protein. A *choinix* of barley meal will provide 2,320 calories, but when cooked and digested as bread it contains only 1,897 usable calories and 63g of protein (Foxhall-Forbes, 1982: Table 3). Modern medical opinion considers (for largely sedentary populations) that 1,750 to 1,950 calories and around 55g of protein are sufficient for a civilian male, while 3,250 calories as a reasonable minimum should sustain a soldier. However, we have to remember that an ancient soldier tended to be older, smaller, and more inured to hardship than those of modern western armies. Foxhall and Forbes point out that according to UN Food and Agriculture Organization standards 'a man aged 20–39, weighing 62kg, would require… only 2,853 calories per day if he were moderately active', and argue this would be the man of ancient Greece (1982: 56). By this reckoning, therefore, our ancient soldier would derive some 66.5 per cent of his energy needs from consuming his daily bread. For men undertaking arduous physical work, carbohydrates (namely bread) were obviously crucial. Fats (namely dairy and olive products) keep out the cold, but protein, though desirable, could wait for a while.

Attic helmet (London, British Museum, GR 1883.12-8.3), late 5th century BC. With good ventilation, hearing and vision without sacrificing too much facial protection, this had been a very popular helmet in its original 'Chalcidian' form, especially in southern Italy and Sicily. However, improved versions with a cranial ridge for better protection and hinged cheek pieces for better ventilation appeared. The nasal guard also became smaller and disappeared entirely from some helmets, giving rise to the Attic style in which the only vestige of the nasal piece was an inverted V over the brow. (Fields-Carré Collection)

EXPERIENCE OF BATTLE

Among the most important truisms of war is that an army is rooted in a fragile psychology that is far more vital than either organization or technology. All men are brave, and all men are cowards, depending on the circumstances. A man can call upon his heart for courage but the result may not be what he wants. Indeed, the instinct to stay put and kill comes with experience; it is not taught. In its rawest form it is a man's natural fear of losing his reputation as a man among his immediate comrades that armours him against the terrible experience of battle. We, who in our everyday lives are always governed by the dictates of self-preservation, cannot begin to understand what appears to be a grotesque willingness to die. Yet old hands know what it is like to submit themselves to the pitiless ordeal of combat again and again more or less willingly, to pass the dividing line beyond which the instinct of self-preservation ceases to exist. To do otherwise is to disgrace themselves in front of their fellow soldiers whose esteem is the foundation of their own self-respect. Men will kill and die rather than lose face – the face, that is, of the tribal warrior of man's pre-civilized past who fought for personal glory and stood a very good chance of surviving to fight another day.

It remains a matter of record that the vast mass of men, even men born and nurtured in enlightened and protective societies, can become killers if the right stimuli are applied. Removed from a comfortable peacetime routine and trained in the same hard school, we too might be like them ourselves. The lesson can be only that there simply is no inherent prohibition against the taking of life built into the human psyche. The inhibitions are all external, and in time of war they are carefully removed to expose the ingrained warrior ethic. On that ancient level, add self-confidence and professional skill, add resource, cunning, no nonsense about fair play, a strong disregard for human life and suffering – especially the other man's – and we have a competent and effective professional soldier.

This is why 'old soldiers' are best; they have the ability to take care of themselves and survive the longest. The longer a man survives, the more battles he wins; the more he wins, the deeper the killer instinct is graven upon his nature. Training for war is a means to an end and the real measure of any true professional soldier is his experience of that central act of war: battle. Training transforms a raw recruit into a trained soldier, but battle (if he survives both mentally and physically) matures a soldier quickly and elevates him to veteran status. Battle is the proverbial 'baptism of fire' that will eventually turn soldiers into a finely honed fighting instrument. The

G — DESTRUCTION OF THE SACRED BAND, THE KRIMISOS 341 BC

'To the inexperienced battle is pleasant, but he who has had experience of it, in his heart he sorely fears its approach', wrote the Theban poet Pindar (*Dance Songs*, 110). In the mayhem of the battlefield many formations did not charge straight into hand-to-hand combat. It took a great deal of bravery and brass to go those last few metres, and they often paused, yelling abuse at the foe. When two sides did slam together, what happened was quite impersonal. Opposing front ranks were often crushed hard against each other by the press of those behind, lunging with spears over the heads and shoulders of their comrades. There, in such close proximity, a fatal blow might equally come from a blade in an unseen hand as from a spear. In other places the battle lines stood a spear-length apart, searching furiously with the points of their spears for a crippling strike – a thigh, a groin, a throat, an armpit exposed by an outstretched arm – while fending off the thrusts of their adversaries. Though it was a pair of fighters who stabbed or slashed at each other with spear or sword before one or the other went down, there was nothing personal in the exchange. Here, we do not witness the choreographic encounters of bright shining heroes.

In this adrenalin fuelled tête-à-tête the shield provided vital protection, and the fighter feared losing his footing almost as much as a disabling blow. It mattered little whether he was brought low by the thrusting strike of a spear, or the muscle-tearing cut of a well-directed sword; once felled, he was horribly vulnerable and likely to be trampled to death. His only hope lay in scuttling away between the legs of those behind and leaving this grim abattoir as fast as he was able. If his side were to give up, thereby abandoning the fight in favour of flight, he knew that he stood more chance of being hacked down and hurried on to Hades. And so it was on that awful storm-torn morning by the Krimesos.

In this plate we witness the fleeing Carthaginian survivors slipping and sliding in a quagmire of mud, some throwing themselves aside beyond the arc of the slashing swords, as the victorious Greeks give chase. Fear and horror can be seen on faces streaked by rain and sweat. Once one side has flinched and panic has taken hold, the vanquished suffer fearful losses in the initial rout. Its wake is dotted with arms and equipment cast down on the battlefield, and many of the pursuers have stopped to gather loot. Scattered in broken heaps on the summer mud are the dead and wounded. Many more have drowned in the swollen river. So died the Sacred Band of Carthage.

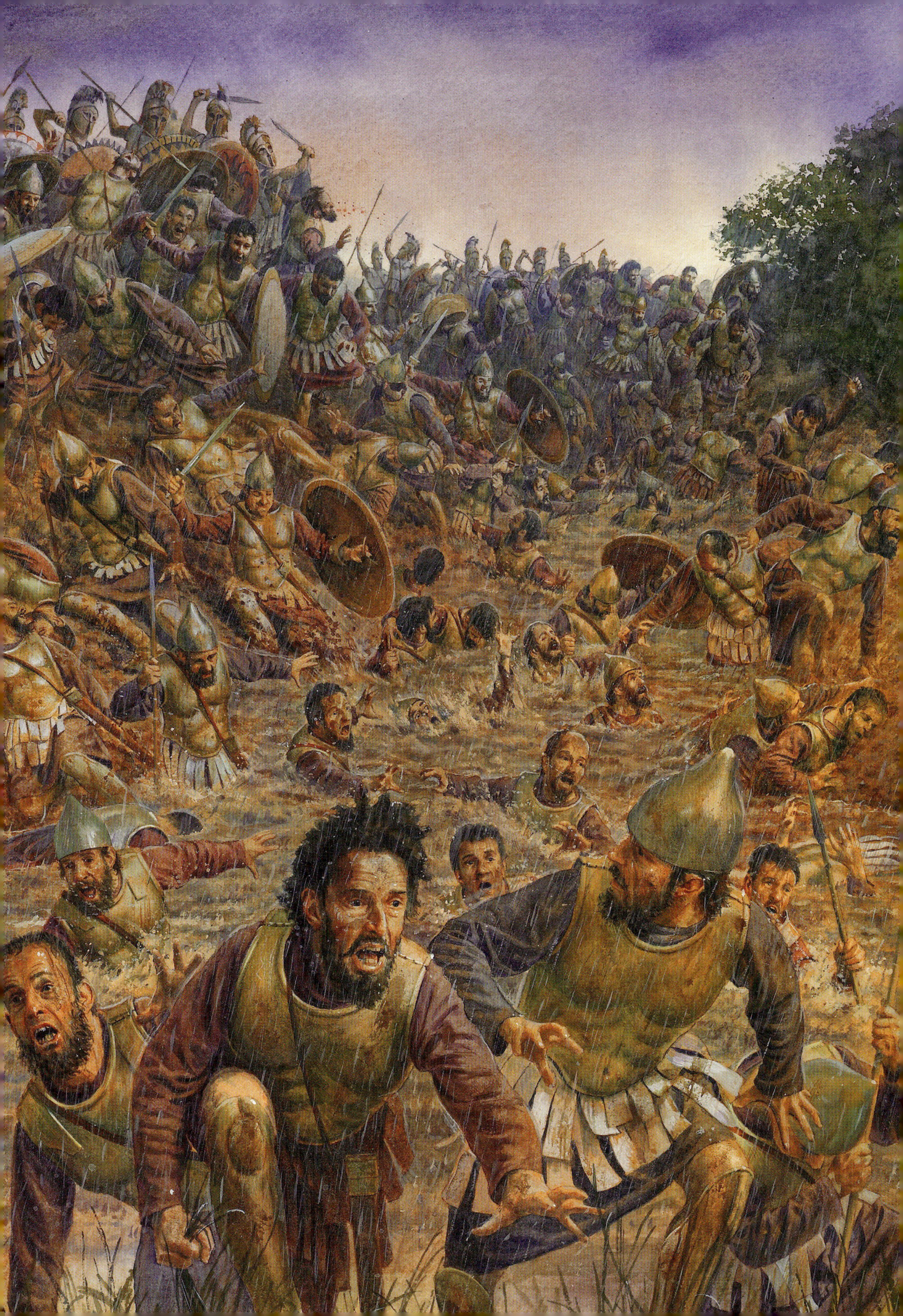

ABOVE LEFT AND RIGHT Iberian *falcata* (top) and Greek *kopis* (bottom), both from Almedinilla, Córdoba, 4th century BC (Madrid, Museo Arqueológico Nacional, 10470, 10475). The *kopis* was a single-edged blade that widened towards the point, moving its centre of gravity farther forward, thereby increasing the kinetic energy of a downward, cutting blow. The *falcata*, which derived from the *kopis*, was occasionally sharpened on the back edge near the point to enable it to thrust as well as cut, as clearly seen here. Both have hilts that were forged as one piece with the blade, and curve back to guard the knuckles. These two are in the form of a horse's head, that of the *kopis* richly decorated with silver inlay. The missing insets would have been of organic material, probably bone or ivory. Note the two suspension rings attached to the scabbard frame of the *falcata*, and the engraving of a bird near the point of the *kopis*. (Fields-Carré Collection)

mercenary armies of Carthage would have contained their ample share of 'old soldiers'.

In a conflict of masses, success depends upon the subordination of self to the will of the group. Yet it is within the arena of the battlefield that a soldier, even an 'old soldier', witnesses the greatest violence in war. For him it is a wildly unstable physical and emotional environment; a world of boredom and bewilderment (which makes up the great part of the ordinary soldier's experience), of triumph and terror, of anger and angst, of courage and cowardice. And for the mercenary of Carthage this was the chaotic world where he earned his daily bread. Such men have no voices that reach us clearly.

Archilochos of Paros (fr. 1), who declared himself to be both a servant of lord Ares and of the lovely Muses, spent most of his life as a professional soldier until he was killed in battle sometime in the mid-7th century BC. His poetry is concerned with his personal circumstances – war and battle, love and sex, food and drink – and so offers us a rare, intimate glance into the way of life and death of a workaday mercenary. Therefore a spear can bring death, enrich or satisfy: 'In my spear is my daily bread, in my spear my Ismaric wine, on my spear I lean and drink' (fr. 2). Whatever his reasons for becoming a mercenary, his priorities are often very similar to most others once he has settled into the new way of life. Generally they are concerned with problems of finding food, shelter, a dry bed, alcohol and women, and with staying alive until another day has passed. Soldiering brings out many things in a man, good and bad, but above all it makes him measurelessly down to earth.

Let us now return to the theme of the advantages of the professional over the amateur. Both Plutarch (*Timoleon*, 28.6) and Diodoros (16.81.3, 4) agree that it was the debacle on the banks of the Krimisos that motivated Carthage to look to Greece as a potential source of mercenaries. Both, too, report the city's utter shock over the fearful loss of so many of its brave citizens, Diodoros going so far as to add that a decree was hurriedly passed that curtailed the practice of sending overseas a body of citizen soldiers as Carthage had done to Sicily with fatal results. Despite unexpected aid from the elements, Timoleon's victory was owed to the superior discipline and experience of the Greek mercenaries in his army, for Carthage had in its citizenry soldiers whose primary function was to fight at close quarters in a well-drilled phalanx.

In their respective accounts of the battle, Plutarch (*Timoleon*, 27.3, 28.1, 3) and Diodoros (16.80.3, 6) both say that the citizens were well protected by corselets, helmets and large shields, and unpublished stelae from Carthage are described as depicting similar soldiers in muscled cuirasses, conical helmets and round shields (Head, 1982: 140–2). The conical-style helmet, usually in bronze, was a common pattern in the east, used by the armies of Assyria, Persia and so on, and an iron example was recovered from a 2nd-century BC Numidian prince's tomb at el-Soumâa. Body armour in the form of stiff linen was worn too, since Pausanias saw three linen corselets at Olympia, describing them as 'the dedication of Gelon and the Syracusans after overpowering the Phoenicians (*Phoínikas*) either in a land or sea battle' (6.19.4). Pausanias probably saw an inscription on the objects, which marked them as war spoils taken from the 'Phoenicians' (i.e. Carthaginians) by Gelon of Syracuse, perhaps at Himera (480 BC). Additionally, Diodoros says (16.80.2) that the citizen soldiers at Krimisos were armed with spears and, though we are uncertain of the spear's length in comparison to the long thrusting spear carried by a hoplite, Plutarch does mention that 'the struggle came to swords' (*Timoleon*, 28.2), which does suggest that a Carthaginian citizen was not materially inferior to a Greek hoplite. For what it is worth, the above-mentioned stelae apparently show broad-bladed spears as long as their bearers are high, which makes the spear of a Carthaginian shorter than that of a Greek, the latter being some 2–2.5m in length. In a sense the *dóru*, as the Greeks knew it, was their 'national' weapon. Others, such as the Etruscans and Romans, borrowed it, but no other peoples used it with the confident ferocity of the Greeks.

Of course, Greece was not the only source of mercenaries for Carthage. Fighting with their native weapons, the mercenaries from the Balearic Islands were employed as skirmishers armed with slings, the accurate use of which the islanders were renowned for (Strabo, 3.5.1; Diodoros, 5.18.3–5; Florus, *Epitome*, 1.43.5; Vegetius, 1.16); their role was to open the hostilities, and then to irritate the enemy during the various stages of the battle. The mercenaries from the Iberian peninsula, on the other hand, were armed with either the *falcata* or the straight-bladed weapon with parallel edges and a tapered, sharp point, while those from Celtic lands wielded the long, blunt-pointed sword that was effective only in sweeping, slashing blows. The first were close-fighting warriors, and the second adopted a much looser formation, yet both nonetheless carried spears and javelins.

Generally, these fighters were composed of ordinary, free tribesmen who were able to equip themselves. They would have formed loose war bands

Reverse of a Punic silver coin (London, British Museum) from the Mogente Hoard, Valencia, dated *c*.230 BC. Minted in southern Iberia by the Barca family, it depicts the elephant regularly employed by the Carthaginians. The African forest elephant (*Loxodonta africana cyclotis*) was smaller than the Indian species – 2.15m to 2.45m tall at the shoulder compared with 3m, and it carried a single rider, not a howdah – but was much easier to train than today's African bush elephant. (Fields-Carré Collection)

H STREET FIGHTING, CARTHAGE 146 BC

In the spring of 146 BC Scipio Aemilianus gave the orders for the final attack. The last agony of Carthage was at hand. By now, the shortage of food had taken its toll in the city, and when the Romans launched a savage and slaughterous assault from the harbour area, where they had established themselves the previous autumn, a stretch of the city wall fell after brief resistance. Thence they advanced without difficulty to the agora, while the defenders fled to the Byrsa, and here the last, desperate, half-starved remnant held out.

Tall houses along narrow lanes proved to be individual strongholds, and the fighting was house-to-house, floor-to-floor, room-to-room and hand-to-hand for six days while the war-torn city below them burnt and resounded to the shouts of the victors as they looted and pillaged. The account given by Appian, which gives a graphic description of the bitter street fighting, was probably taken from Polybios, whose own eyewitness record has been largely lost:

> There were three streets ascending from the agora to this fortress [the Byrsa], along which, on either side, were houses built closely together and six storeys high, from which the Romans were assailed with missiles. They were compelled, therefore, to possess themselves of the first ones and use those as a means of expelling the occupants from the next. When they had mastered the first, they threw timbers from one to another over the narrow passageways, and crossed as on bridges. While battle was waging in this way on the roofs, another fight was going on among those who met each other in the streets below. All places were filled with groans, shrieks, shouts, and every kind of agony. Some were stabbed, others were hurled alive from the roofs to the pavement, some of them alighting on the heads of spears or other pointed weapons, or swords. No one dared to set fire to the houses on account of those who were still on the roofs, until Scipio reached the Byrsa. Then he set fire to the streets all together, and gave orders to keep the passageways clear of burning material so that the army might move back and forth freely.

On the seventh day the citadel surrendered, and 50,000 men and women apparently came forth to slavery. For ten more days the fires of Carthage raged. Finally, the ruins were razed, a plough was symbolically drawn over the site and salt sown in the furrows, and a solemn curse was pronounced against its future rebirth. Carthage had been destroyed.

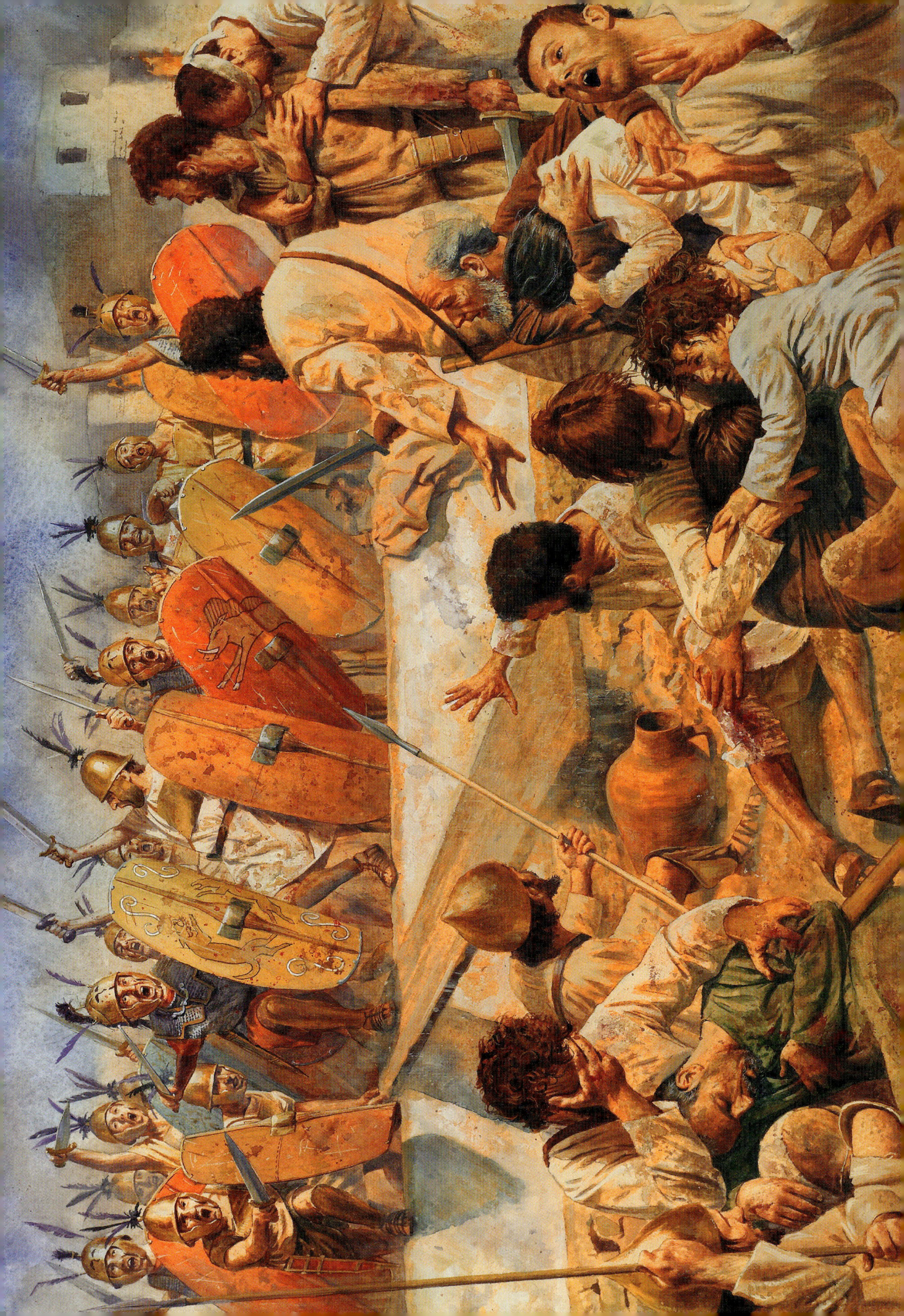

based on clan, familiar, and settlement groupings, making a man's people the witness of his behaviour. Tactics were simple and relied on a wild, headlong rush by a yelling mass of warriors in a rough phalangial order headed by their war leaders, followed up by deadly close work with spear and sword. As is common in tribal contingents, the warriors were poorly disciplined and lacked training above the level of the individual. And so after a violent and savage onslaught launched amid a colossal din, the individual warrior battered his way into the enemy's ranks punching with his shield. What had been two distinct bodies of men was now an intermingled, heaving mass of men stabbing and slashing at each other with spear and sword. On the whole, battle for these warriors seems to have consisted of a general mêlée with the principal concern being to knock hell out of the opposition in whatever manner was most effective.

As for the Libyans, all we can say for certain is that by Hannibal's day, at any rate, they were worse armed than Roman soldiers. Polybios says (3.87.3, 114.1) that Hannibal issued his Libyans with Roman war gear plundered from the booty of the Trebbia and Lake Trasimene, and Livy notes (22.46.4) that thereafter they could easily have been mistaken for actual Romans. But does this mean the Libyans re-equipped themselves only with Roman helmets, body armour, greaves and *scuta*, or did they take *pila* and *gladii* too? If the latter, then we have to assume the Libyans were trained, like Roman legionaries, as swordsmen, since it is unlikely that Hannibal would

The year 146 BC marks, or symbolizes at least, the end of an era. History is never as neat and tidy as that, of course, but the date is not entirely arbitrary. The year 146 BC has an air of culmination about it, with two illustrious cities, Punic Carthage and Greek Corinth, destroyed and plundered by the soldiers of Rome. Here we see the ruins of the citadel of Byrsa, Punic Carthage, with Cap Bon or Rass Adder, the ancient Hermaia Promontory, in the far distance. (Ancient Art & Architecture)

have risked retraining his best infantry in the course of a campaign (Lazenby, 1978: 14, cf. Bagnall, 1999: 170). Besides, extensive, uninterrupted training time was a luxury that the Libyans simply did not have.

Tentative evidence against their adoption of Roman weaponry comes from Plutarch, in a passage referring to a period after the adoption of Roman legionary equipment, when he says that 'Carthaginians were not trained in throwing the javelin and carried only short spears for hand-to-hand fighting' (*Marcellus*, 12.8). Naturally Plutarch uses the term 'javelin' (*akóntion* in his Greek), but probably said this with *pilum* in mind. Also, for 'Carthaginians' read 'Libyan spearmen', because in the same breath Plutarch talks of Iberians and Numidians deserting to Marcellus, and we know from the much more reliable Polybios that Libyans and Iberians made up the bulk of Hannibal's infantry force (e.g. 3.56.1). In other words, just prior to contact with Roman legionaries, Carthaginian spearmen would have to endure a lethal hail of *pila* to which they had no response. However, we quickly notice that in this passage Plutarch makes reference only to the *pilum*, not to the *gladius*. Prior to Italy the Libyans had fought in Iberia under the Barca family for nigh on two decades, and it is possible that they had adopted that very efficient Iberian cut-and-thrust sword from which it is believed the Roman *gladius* developed (Daly, 2002: 90).

GLOSSARY

* *Akóntion*	javelin
† *Caetra*	small, round buckler of Iberian origin
* *Choinix*	dry measure equivalent of a man's daily grain ration (Attic *choinix* = 1.08kg)
Cubit	unit of measurement equal to the length from the elbow to the tip of the little finger (Attic cubit = 444mm)
Cuir bouilli	'boiled leather' – leather soaked in cold water, moulded into shape, and dried hard using a low heat
† *Falcata*	curved, single-edged Iberian sword derived from the Greek kopis (q.v.)
† *Gladius*	Roman sword with broad blade and tapered stabbing point
Hoplite	heavily-armed foot soldier accustomed to fighting shoulder-to-shoulder in a phalanx
* *Kopis*	curved, single-edged, heavy slashing-type sword of Greek origin
† *Libra*	Roman pound (= 327.17g)
* *Longche*	light spear
* *Medimnos*	dry measure equal to 48 Attic *choinikes* (q.v.)

† *Pilum*		principal throwing weapon of Roman legionaries
* *Pteruges*		'feathers' – strip defences usually of stiff linen or hardened leather
† *Pugio*		broad-bladed dagger carried by Roman legionaries
* *Saunion*		javelin
† *Scutum*		flat oval body shield of Italic origin
† *Soliferreum*		all-iron javelin of Iberian origin
Span		unit of measurement equal to the distance across a man's outstretched hand (= 223mm)
Stater		gold coin equivalent to 20–28 drachmae depending on the time and place (e.g. Attic stater = 20 drachmae, a drachma being six obolos)

* = Greek term

† = Latin term

BIBLIOGRAPHY

Austin, M. M., *The Hellenistic world from Alexander to the Roman conquest: A selection of ancient sources in translation* (Cambridge University Press: Cambridge, 1981)

Bagnall, N., *The Punic Wars: Rome, Carthage and the Struggle for the Mediterranean* (Pimlico: London, 1990)

Bath, T., *Hannibal's Campaigns* (Patrick Stephens: Cambridge, 1981)

Beer, G. de, *Hannibal's March* (Sidgwick & Jackson: London, 1967)

——, *Hannibal* (Thames & Hudson: London, 1969)

Braudel, F., *The Mediterranean World in the Ancient World* (Penguin: London, 1998)

Brett, M. and Fentress, E. W. B., *The Berbers* (Blackwell: Oxford, 1996)

Burstein, S. M., *Translated Documents of Greece and Rome 3: The Hellenistic Age from the battle of Ipsos to the death of Kleopatra VII* (Cambridge University Press: Cambridge, 1985)

Camps, G., *Aux origines de la Berbérie: monuments et rites funéraires protohistoriques* (Arts et métiers graphiques: Paris, 1962)

Carey, B. T., Allfree, J. B. and Cairns, J., *Warfare in the Ancient World* (Pen & Sword: Barnsley, 2005)

Connolly, P., *Greece and Rome at War* (Macdonald Phoebus: London, 1981)

Cornell, T. J., Rankov, N. B. and Sabin, P. (eds.), *The Second Punic War: A Reappraisal* (University of London Press: London, 1996)

Daly, G., *Cannae: The Experience of Battle in the Second Punic War* (Routledge: London, 2002)

Engels, D. W., *Alexander the Great and the Logistics of the Macedonian Army* (University of California Press: Berkeley, 1978)

Everson, T., *Warfare in Ancient Greece: Arms and Armour from the Heroes of*

Homer to Alexander the Great (Sutton: Stroud, 2004)
Feugère, M., *Les armes romains de la république à l'antiquité tardive* (Editions du Centre national de la recherche scientifique: Paris, 1993)
Fields, N., *The Roman Army of the Punic Wars 264–146 BC* (Osprey: Oxford, 2007)
Foxhall, L. and Forbes, H. A., 'Σιτομετρεία: the role of grain as a staple food in classical antiquity' in *Chiron* 12, pp.41–90 (1982)
Goldsworthy, A. K., *The Roman Army at War 100 BC–AD 200* (Clarendon Press: Oxford, 1996)
——, *The Punic Wars* (Cassell: London, 2000)
——, *Cannae* (Cassell: London, 2001)
Griffith, G. T., *The Mercenaries of the Hellenistic World* (Cambridge University Press: Cambridge, 1935)
Gsell, S., *Histoire ancienne de l'Afrique du Nord*, vol. 2 (Paris, 1928)
Harding, P., *Translated Documents of Greece and Rome 2: From the end of the Peloponnesian War to the battle of Ipsus* (Cambridge University Press: Cambridge, 1985)
Harris, H. A., 'Greek javelin throwing' in *Greece & Rome* 10, pp.26–36 (1963)
Head, D., *Armies of the Macedonian and Punic Wars 359 BC–146 BC* (Wargames Research Group: Worthing, 1982)
Hoyos D., *Hannibal's Dynasty: Power and Politics in the Western Mediterranean, 247–183 BC* (Routledge: London, 2003)
Jones, B. W., 'Rome's relationship with Carthage: a study in aggression' in *The Classical Bulletin* 49, pp.5–26 (1972)
Kistler, J. M. de, *War Elephants* (Praeger Publishers: Westport, CT, 2005)
Lancel, S., *Carthage* (Oxford University Press: Oxford, 1995)
Lazenby, J. F., *Hannibal's War: A Military History of the Second Punic War* (Aris & Phillips: Warminster, 1978)
——, 'Logistic in Classical Greek Warfare' in *War in History* 1 (1): 3–18 (1994)
——, *The First Punic War: A Military History* (University College London Press: London, 1996)
Moscati, S. (ed.), *The Phoenicians* (I. B. Tauris: London, 1997)
Nossov, K. S., *War Elephants* (Osprey: Oxford, 2008)
Parke, H. W., *Greek Mercenary Soldiers: From the Earliest Times to the Battle of Ipsus* (Clarendon Press: Oxford, 1933)
Picard, C. G. and Picard, C., (trans. D. Collon, 1969), *The Life and Death of Carthage* (Sidgwick & Jackson: London, 1968)
Proctor, D., *Hannibal's March in History* (Clarendon Press: Oxford, 1971)
Rawlings, L., 'Celts, Spanish and Samnites: Warriors in a Soldier's War' in *The Second Punic War: A Reappraisal* (University of London Press: London, 1996)
Sage, M. M., *Warfare in Ancient Greece: A Sourcebook* (Routledge: London, 1996)
Sekunda, N., *Greek Hoplite 480–323 BC* (Osprey, Oxford, 2000)
Scullard, H. H., *The Elephant in the Greek and Roman World (*Thames & Hudson: London, 1974)
Seibert, J., *Hannibal* (Wissenschaftliche Buchgesellschaft: Darmstadt, 1993)
Snodgrass, A. M., *Early Greek Armour and Weapons* (Edinburgh University Press: Edinburgh, 1965)
Spring, C., *African Arms and Armour* (British Museum Press: London, 1993)
Warry, J., *Warfare in the Classical World* (Salamander: London, 1980)
Wilcox, P. and Treviño, R., *Barbarians against Rome: Rome's Celtic, Germanic, Spanish and Gallic Enemies* (Osprey: Oxford, 2000)
Wise T. and Healy, M., *Hannibal's War with Rome: The Armies and Campaigns 216 BC* (Osprey: Oxford, 1999)

INDEX

Figures in **bold** refer to illustrations

Achaian League 43
Aeneid **14**
Agathokles 19–20, 27, 30–31
appearance
    Balearic slingers **C (25)**
    citizen soldiers **A (17)**, **C (25)**, 57
    Gaulish/Celtic warriors 34, **36**, **37**
    Greek hoplites 43
    Iberian warriors **18**, **B (21)**, 27, **36**
    Libyan warriors **C (24)**
    Oscan warriors **F (45)**
    overview 31–32
    Samnite warriors **26**
    Spartan warriors **E (41)**
    see also armour; helmets
Appian 58
Aratos 43
Archilochos 46, 49, 56
Aristophanes 48
Aristotle 12, **13**, 14, 15
armour
    greaves **36**, 43, **F (45)**
    linen **A (17)**, 57
    metal **B (21)**, **26**, 32, **33**, **35**, **E (41)**, **F (45)**
    overview 32
    quilted 27, **36**
Autaritos 23

Baetis, battle of the (229 BC) **B (21)**
Balearic warriors **C (25)**, 43, 58
Barca family: soldier loyalty to 24
Bomilcar 13

Cannae, battle of (216 BC) 22, 24–26
Carthage **4**, **5**
    colonies 5–6
    constitution 12–15
    foundation and history 4–6
    Roman capture (146 BC) **H (59)**, 60
Cato, Marcus Porcius 5
cavalry **22**
Celtic warriors *see* Gaulish warriors
cereal types 48–49
Cicero 15
citizen soldiers 14–15, 16–18, **A (17)**
    see also Sacred Band

Dido 12, **14**
Diodoros Siculus 16, 19, 24, 56–58

Ebusus, battle of (206 BC) **C (25)**
elephants **50**, 51, 58
Eryx 23

Florus 4, 24, 50
food and rations 46–52

Gaulish warriors
    appearance and equipment **22**, 34, **36**, **37**, 48, 58
    in Sicily 23
    generals: scrutiny and freedom of command 12–14
    Greek hoplites 19–20, **23**, 30–31, **43**, 57–58

Hamilcar 19–20, 23, 24, 30
Hannibal **51**, **52**
    acclamation as general 15, 24
    army's composition 19, 23–24, 60–61
    at Cannae 22, 24–26
    desertion of mercenaries from 31
    recruitment procedures 28
    at Zama 16
Hanno **D (29)**
Hasdrubal 24
Hekatompylos 28
helmets
    Attic **26**, 53
    conical-style 57
    Iberian **22**
    Montefortino **31**, **F (45)**
    Phrygian **15**, **A (17)**
    pilos **E (41)**
    'Thracian' **32**, 43
Himilco 19

Iberian warriors
    appearance and equipment **18**, **B (21)**, **22**, 27, **36**, 58
    desertions 31
    military prowess 18

Jason of Pherai 20–22
jewellery **12**

killer instinct 53–56
Krimisos, battle of the (341 BC) 16, 19, **G (55)**, 56–58

Libyan War (240–237 BC) 23, 27–28, **D (29)**, 44, 51
Libyan warriors
    appearance and equipment **C (25)**, **D (29)**, 47, 60–61
    loyalty 23–24, 27–28
    military prowess 24–26
Lilybaeum, siege of 22–23
Livy 13, 31, 60

Mago 19, 24
mercenaries
    advantages 56–58
    organization and tactics 58–60
    overview 18–26
    paying 43–44
    recruitment 28–31
    see also individual ethnic types by name
Metaurus, battle of the (207 BC) 51

Naravas 30
Numidian warriors 28–30, 31

Onasander 42
Oscan belts **26**, 49
Oscan warriors 31–32, **F (45)**

Paullus, Lucius Aemilius 22
Pausanias 57
pay 44–46
Philon of Byzantium 38
Pindar 54
Plato 51

plunder 46
Plutarch 16, 18, 19, 51–57, 58, 61
Polybios
    on Balearic slingers 24
    on Cannae 22
    on Carthage's constitution 15
    on First Punic War 23
    on Hannibal's army 24, 60, 61
    on Hanno 28
    on Libyan War 27–28, 44–46, 51
    on soldiers' rations 48, 49, 52
    on swords 36–38
    on Xanthippos 40
    on Zama 16, 44

recruitment 26–31
religion 6, **12**
Roman legionaries 47, 48, 49

Sacred Band 16–18, 19, 43, **G (55)**, 57–58
Samnite warriors **26**
Scipio, Cnaeus Cornelius 31
Scipio Aemilianus, Publius Cornelius 58
shields
    aspis 23
    caetra 19, **B (21)**, 27, 30, **36**, 43
    Gaulish **22**, 34
    scutarus **18**
    scutum **F (45)**
Sicily
    Carthaginian power 6
    Hamilcar in 19–20
    the Krimisos 16, 19, **G (55)**, 56–58
    and the Punic Wars 22–23, 44
Spartan warriors **E (41)**
swords
    Gaulish/Celtic 14, 34, **36**–**38**, 48
    Iberian *falcata* **18**, **B (21)**, **C (25)**, 35, **36**, **37**, 56–**57**
    kopis **A (17)**, 56–**57**
    overview 35–38

Teuta, queen of Illyria 23
Thucydides 18
Timaios (of Tauromenion) 5
Timoleon 16, 19, 31, 57
Trebbia, battle of the (218 BC) 51–52
Tunis, battle of (255 BC) **E (41)**

Varro, Caius Terentius 13
Vegetius 24, 35–36

weapons
    daggers **B (21)**, **C (25)**, 35, **37**, **38**–**39**, **38**
    javelins **B (21)**, **22**, 39–42, **39**
    Libyan 60–61
    overview 31–43
    slings and shots **C (25)**, **39**, 42–43, **42**
    spears **A (17)**, 32–34, 57–58
    see also swords

Xanthippos 30, **E (41)**
Xenophon 43, 49, 50–51

Zama, battle of (202 BC) **A (17)**, 24, **F (45)**